W9-ABR-878

Sadlier

Grade One

Sadlier

A Division of William H. Sadlier, Inc.

Nihil Obstat
Reverend John G. Stillmank, S.T.L.
Censor Librorum

Imprimatur
✠ Most Reverend William H. Bullock
Bishop of Madison
November 25, 2002

The *Nihil Obstat* and *Imprimatur* are official declarations that a book or pamphlet is free of doctrinal or moral error. No implication is contained therein that those who have granted the *Nihil Obstat* and *Imprimatur* agree with the contents, opinions, or statements expressed.

Acknowledgments

Excerpts from the English translation of the *Catechism of the Catholic Church* for the United States of America, copyright © 1994, United States Catholic Conference, Inc.—Libreria Editrice Vaticana. English translation of the *Catechism of the Catholic Church: Modifications from the Editio Typica* copyright © 1997, United States Catholic Conference, Inc.—Libreria Editrice Vaticana. Used with permission.

Scripture excerpts are taken from the *New American Bible* with *Revised New Testament and Psalms* Copyright © 1991, 1986, 1970, Confraternity of Christian Doctrine, Inc., Washington, D.C. Used with permission. All rights reserved. No part of the *New American Bible* may be reproduced by any means without permission in writing from the copyright owner.

Excerpts from the English translation of *Rite of Baptism for Children* © 1969, International Committee on English in the Liturgy, Inc. (ICEL); excerpts from the English translation of *Lectionary for Mass* © 1969, 1981, ICEL; excerpts from the English translation of *The Roman Missal* © 1973, ICEL; excerpts from the English translation of *Rite of Penance* © 1974, ICEL; excerpts from the English translation of *A Book of Prayers* © 1982, ICEL; excerpts from the English translation of *Book of Blessings* © 1988, ICEL. All rights reserved.

English translation of the Glory to the Father, Lord's Prayer, Apostles' Creed by the International Consultation on English Texts. (ICET)

Tracking online life: How women use the Internet to cultivate relationships with family and friends. Pew Internet & American Life Project, May 2000. Used with permission.

Excerpt from America's Children: Key National Indicators of Well-Being, 1999. Prepared by the Federal Interagency Forum on Child and Family Statistics.

Excerpt *Times to Remember*, by Rose Fitzgerald Kennedy, © 1974, Doubleday, a division of Random House, Inc. Used with permission.

"We Believe, We Believe in God," © 1979, North American Liturgy Resources (NALR), 5536 NE Hassalo, Portland, OR 97213. All rights reserved. Used with permission. "People Worry," © 1993, Daughters of Charity and Christopher Walker. Published by OCP Publications, 5536 NE Hassalo, Portland, OR 97213. All rights reserved. Used with permission. "Children of God," Michael B. Lynch. Copyright © 1977, Raven Music. All rights reserved. Used with permission. "Jesus Wants to Help Us," music and text © 1999, Christopher Walker and Paule Freeburg, DC. Published by OCP Publications, 5536 NE Hassalo, Portland, OR 97213. All rights reserved. Used with permission. "In the House of Our God," © 1988, 1989, 1990, Christopher Walker. Published by OCP Publications, 5536 NE Hassalo, Portland, OR 97213. All rights reserved. Used with permission. "Sing for Joy," © 1999, Bernadette Farrell. Published by OCP Publications, 5536 NE Hassalo,

Portland, OR 97213. All rights reserved. Used with permission. "Share the Light," © 1999, Bernadette Farrell. Published by OCP Publications, 5536 NE Hassalo, Portland, OR 97213. All rights reserved. Used with permission. "We Are the Church," © 1991, Christopher Walker. Published by OCP Publications, 5536 NE Hassalo, Portland, OR 97213. All rights reserved. Used with permission. "We Are the Church" was originally from "Come, Follow Me" Music Program, Benziger Publishing Company. "Advent Song," Words/Music by MaryLu Walker © 1975, 1998, 16 Brown Road, Corning, New York 14830. All rights reserved. Used with permission. "Jesus, Come to Us," © 1981, 1982, OCP Publications, 5536 NE Hassalo, Portland, OR 97213. All rights reserved. Used with permission. "Open Our Hearts," © 1989, Christopher Walker. Published by OCP Publications, 5536 NE Hassalo, Portland, OR 97213. All rights reserved. Used with permission. "We Celebrate with Joy," © 2000, Carey Landry. Published by OCP Publications, 5536 NE Hassalo, Portland, OR 97213. All rights reserved. Used with permission. "Celebrate God," © 1973, North American Liturgy Resources (NALR), 5536 NE Hassalo, Portland, OR 97213. All rights reserved. Used with permission. "Walk in the Light," © 1996, Carey Landry. Published by OCP Publications, 5536 NE Hassalo, Portland, OR 97213. All rights reserved. Used with permission. "Children of God," © 1991, Christopher Walker. Published by OCP Publications, 5536 NE Hassalo, Portland, OR 97213. All rights reserved. Used with permission. "Awake, Arise and Rejoice!" © 1992, Marie-Jo Thum. Published by OCP Publications, 5536 NE Hassalo, Portland, OR 97213. All rights reserved. Used with permission. "Shout From the Mountains," © 1992, Marie-Jo Thum. Published by OCP Publications, 5536 NE Hassalo, Portland, OR 97213. All rights reserved. Used with permission. "We Come to Share God's Special Gift," © 1991, Christopher Walker. Published by OCP Publications, 5536 NE Hassalo, Portland, OR 97213. All rights reserved. Used with permission. "Walk in Love," © 1990, North American Liturgy Resources (NALR), 5536 NE Hassalo, Portland, OR 97213. All rights reserved. Used with permission. "Joseph Was a Good Man," music and text © 1999, Christopher Walker and Paule Freeburg, DC. Published by OCP Publications, 5536 NE Hassalo, Portland, OR 97213. All rights reserved. Used with permission. "Malo, Malo, Thanks Be to God," © 1993, Jesse Manibusan. Administered by OCP Publications, 5536 NE Hassalo, Portland, OR 97213. All rights reserved. Used with permission. "Alleluia No. 1," Donald Fishel. © 1973, WORD OF GOD MUSIC (Administered by THE COPYRIGHT COMPANY, Nashville, TN). All rights reserved. International copyright secured. Used with permission. "Jesus Wants to Help Us," music and text © 1999, Christopher Walker and Paule Freeburg, DC. Published by OCP Publications, 5536 NE Hassalo, Portland, OR 97213. All rights reserved. Used with permission.

William H. Sadlier, Inc.
9 Pine Street
New York, NY 10005-1002

ISBN: 0-8215-5401-8
23456789/07 06 05 04 03

The Ad Hoc Committee to Oversee the Use of the Catechism,
United States Conference of Catholic Bishops,
has found this catechetical text, copyright 2004,
to be in conformity with the *Catechism of the Catholic Church*.

The Sadlier *We Believe* Program was developed by nationally recognized experts in catechesis, curriculum, and child development. These teachers of the faith and practitioners helped us to frame every lesson to be age-appropriate and appealing. In addition, a team including respected catechetical, liturgical, pastoral, and theological experts shared their insights and inspired the development of the program.

The Program is truly based on the wisdom of the community, including:

Gerard F. Baumbach, Ed.D.
Executive Vice President and Publisher

Carole M. Eipers, D.Min.
Director of Catechetics

Catechetical and Liturgical Consultants

Reverend Monsignor John F. Barry
Pastor, American Martyrs Parish
Manhattan Beach, CA

Sister Linda Gaupin, CDP, Ph.D.
Director of Religious Education
Diocese of Orlando

Mary Jo Tully
Chancellor, Archdiocese of Portland

Reverend Monsignor John M. Unger
Assoc. Superintendent for Religious Education
Archdiocese of St. Louis

Curriculum and Child Development Consultants

Brother Robert R. Bimonte, FSC
Former Superintendent of Catholic Education
Diocese of Buffalo

Gini Shimabukuro, Ed.D.
Associate Director/Associate Professor
Institute for Catholic Educational Leadership
School of Education, University of
San Francisco

Catholic Social Teaching Consultants

John Carr
Secretary, Department of Social Development
and World Peace, USCCB

Joan Rosenhauer
Coordinator, Special Projects
Department of Social Development and
World Peace, USCCB

Inculturation Consultants

Reverend Allan Figueroa Deck, SJ, Ph.D.
Executive Director, Loyola Institute for
Spirituality, Orange, CA

Kirk Gaddy
Principal, St. Katharine School
Baltimore, MD

Reverend Nguyễn Việt Hưng
Vietnamese Catechetical Committee

Dulce M. Jiménez-Abreu
Director of Spanish Programs
William H. Sadlier, Inc.

Contents

UNIT 2 We Are Followers of Jesus

UNIT 3 We Belong to the Church

WE BELIEVE

The *We Believe* program will help us to

learn

celebrate

share

and live our Catholic faith.

Throughout the year we will hear about many saints and holy people.

Saint Andrew Kim Taegon

Saint Anne

Saint Francis of Assisi

Saint Francis Xavier

Saint John Vianney

Saint Joseph

Saint Katharine Drexel

Saint Patrick

Saints Peter and Paul

Pope Pius X

Saint Teresa of Avila

Mother Teresa

Together, let us grow as a community of faith.

Welcome!

✝ We Gather in Prayer

Leader: Welcome everyone to Grade 1 *We Believe*.

As we begin each chapter, we gather in prayer. We pray to God together.

Let us sing the *We Believe* song!

♫ We Believe in God

We believe in God;

We believe, we believe in Jesus;

We believe in the Spirit who gives us life.

We believe, we believe in God.

When we see **We Gather** we come together as a class.

Each day we learn more about God.

WE GATHER

We begin by taking a moment to pray.

✝ *Thank you, God, for our classmates.*

Then we

think about
talk about
write about
draw about
act out

Life

at home
in our neighborhood
at school
in our parish
in our world

Talk about your life right now.

WE BELIEVE

We learn about

- God the Father, God the Son, and God the Holy Spirit
- Jesus, the Son of God, who became one of us
- the Church and its teachings.

We find out about the different ways Catholics live their faith and celebrate God's love.

When we see **We Believe** we learn more about our Catholic faith.

 is an open Bible. When we see it, or something like this (John 13:34), we hear the word of God.

(John 13:34)

✠ means that we will make the sign of the cross and pray as we begin our lesson.

 means it is time to review the important words we have learned in the day's lesson.

means we have an activity. We might

talk   *write*   **act**
draw   **sing**
work together   *imagine*

There are all kinds of activities!

♫ means it's time to sing! We sing songs we know, make up our own songs, and sing along with those in our *We Believe* music program.

Each of these signs points out something special that we are going to do.

As Catholics...

Here we discover something special about our faith. Don't forget to read it!

WE RESPOND

We can respond by

- thinking about ways our faith affects the things we say and do

- sharing our thoughts and feelings

- praying to God.

Then in our homes, neighborhood, school, parish, and world, we can say and do the things that show love for God and others.

 In this space, draw yourself as a *We Believe* first grader.

When we see **We Respond** we think about and act on what we have learned about God and our Catholic faith.

We are so happy you are with us!

14

Review

Here we answer questions about what we have learned in this chapter.

Reflect & Pray

We take a few moments to think about our faith and to pray.

Key Words

We review each of the Key Words.

Review

Grade 1 Chapter 1

Circle the correct answer.

1. All things made by God are _____.

   little   good

2. God created all _____ to know and love him.

   people   animals

3. The Bible is a special _____ about God.

   book   picture

4. God promises to love us _____.

   only at special times   always

 TALK ABOUT IT How can people care for all God's creation?

 ASSESSMENT Make a sign to show some of God's gifts of creation. You might want to draw pictures on it or use pictures from magazines.

We Respond in Faith

Reflect & Pray

Draw or write to finish the prayer. Dear God, I am happy in your wonderful world. I will show you I am happy by

 **Key Words**

creation (p. 21)
Bible (p. 21)

Remember

- God created the world.
- God created all people.
- God gives us special gifts.
- God promises to love us always.

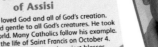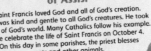 **OUR CATHOLIC LIFE**

Saint Francis of Assisi

Saint Francis loved God and all of God's creation. He was kind and gentle to all God's creatures. He took care of God's world. Many Catholics follow his example. We celebrate the life of Saint Francis on October 4. On this day in some parishes, the priest blesses pets and other animals.

ASSESSMENT

We do a chapter activity that will show that we have discovered more about our Catholic faith.

OUR CATHOLIC LIFE

Here we read an interesting story about the ways people make the world better by living out their Catholic faith.

Remember

We recall the four main faith statements of the chapter.

15

At the end of each chapter, you'll bring a page like this home to share with your family.

Sharing What I Learned

Talk about

WE GATHER

WE BELIEVE   **WE RESPOND**

with your family.

WE BELIEVE
Family Contract

As a **We Believe** family, this year we promise to

_____

_____

Names

_____

_____

_____

GOD LOVES US

A Family Prayer

Lead your family in prayer

People who love us make love grow. Thank you, God, for our family.

People who love us make love grow. Thank you, God, for all the friends of our family.

Most of all, thank you, God, for loving us!

Look here for connections to the Web and to the Catechism.

Visit Sadlier's

www.WEBELIEVEweb.com

Connect to the Catechism of the Catholic Church
For adult background and reflection, Catechism paragraph references are given.

Jesus Teaches Us About God's Love

SHARING FAITH as a Family

What's So Special About Zacchaeus?

The story of Zacchaeus is found in Unit 1. First graders love to hear how Zacchaeus, a despised tax collector, climbed a tree in order to see Jesus. It's one of their favorite biblical stories. No doubt, they know what it feels like to be "little" and have to go to extreme—and undignified—lengths in order to see and be seen. Children of this age are sensitive to being teased. They can relate to the way Zacchaeus was treated by his neighbors.

Jesus' actions in the story can remind parents about treating children with respect:

Children may feel they have to resort to "tree-climbing" techniques in order to get the attention of parents and other significant adults. Be attentive to their feelings and their ideas.

Jesus called Zacchaeus down from the tree and bestowed a great honor on him by going to his house for dinner. Giving children opportunities to shine is important to their sense of self-worth, too.

Zacchaeus explained to Jesus that he was going to give half of his possessions to the poor. Jesus acknowledged Zacchaeus's generosity publicly. Praise your child for his or her acts of kindness. Doing so renews your own sense of appreciation for your child's goodness.

(The entire story of Zacchaeus is found in Luke 19:1–10.)

Note the Quote

"I looked on child rearing not only as a work of love and duty but as a profession that was fully as interesting and challenging as any honorable profession in the world and one that demanded the best that I could bring to it."

—Rose Fitzgerald Kennedy, mother of nine children, including President John F. Kennedy, Senators Robert F. Kennedy and Ted Kennedy

What Your Child Will Learn in Unit 1

In this first unit of the year, the children will be led to understand that Jesus, through his divinity and humanity, teaches us about God's love. The children will recognize that God created the world and everything in it—including them. They will grow in their understanding of the Blessed Trinity. By knowing more about Jesus' family life, the children will become more aware of the blessing of their own families. The last two chapters of the unit focus on Jesus' ministry and teachings. The children begin to see that by his actions of love, mercy and healing, Jesus teaches that God watches over and cares for each of us. The unit concludes with an appreciation of the meaning of Jesus' Great Commandment.

From the Catechism

"Education in the faith by the parents should begin in the child's earliest years."
(Catechism of the Catholic Church, 2226)

Did You Know?

79% of children have at least one parent working full-time, all year.

(America's Children: Key National Indicators of Well-Being, 1999, www.childstats.gov)

A Family Prayer

May the Lord Jesus, who lived with his holy family in Nazareth, dwell also with our family, keep it from evil, and make all of us one in heart and mind.

Amen.

Plan & Preview

▶ Have available construction paper to make a greeting card. *(Sharing Faith with My Family, Chapter 1 Family Page)*

We're so proud of you

TO Nana

I ♥ YOU

God Is Our Father

✝ We Gather in Prayer

Let us show our thanks to God
by singing this song.

🎵 **Thank You, God** *("London Bridge")*

Thank you, God, for Earth, our home.
Earth, our home, Earth, our home.
Thank you, God, for Earth our home.
We say, "Thank you."

Use the same tune to sing about
these gifts in God's world.

- Thank you, God, for birds and fish.
- Thank you, God, for bugs that crawl.
- Thank you, God, for vegetables.
- Thank you, God, for everything.

God created the world.

WE GATHER

✝ *Thank you, God, for our world.*

Look at the picture.
Which things are your favorite?
Tell why.

WE BELIEVE

The word *create* means "to make."
God made everything.
God created our wonderful world.
Creation is everything God made.

Genesis 1:1–31

Read Along

God created light and water. God created fruits and vegetables. God created all kinds of animals.

God created people. Then "God looked at everything he had made, and he found it very good." (Genesis 1:31)

We read about God's creation
in the Bible.
The Bible is a special book
about God.
The **Bible** is the book of God's word.

We believe that God is our Father.
We believe that everything he
created is good.

WE RESPOND

God created our
wonderful world.
What makes the world
so wonderful for you?

Key Words

creation everything
God made

Bible the book of
God's word

 Draw something beautiful
you saw today.

Now pray together.
God, thank you for everything
you made. God, you are wonderful.

God created all people.

WE GATHER

✝ *God, thank you for the gift of creation.*

Name some of your family members. What makes each one special to you?

WE BELIEVE

God wanted to share his love.
So he created people.
We were created to know, love, and serve God.

We are God's special creation.
God did not create everyone to be exactly alike.
Every person is special to God.

God wants people to take care
of his gift of creation.
He wants us to take care
of his world.

How are the people in the pictures
taking care of God's world?

WE RESPOND

What are some ways you can
take care of God's world?

 Draw a picture to finish
this prayer.

God, I take care of your world when I

God gives us special gifts.

WE GATHER

✝ *God our Father, we love you.*

What do plants and animals
do each day?
What do we do?

WE BELIEVE

We can do many things that animals
and plants cannot do.

We can:

- think and learn.
- care for God's world.
- share love with our families
  and friends.
- listen to and talk to God.

These things are gifts from God.
God gives us these gifts so we can
know and love him.

People can help us to do these things.
People are gifts from God, too.
People help us to grow in God's love.

WE RESPOND

Who are the people who help you to grow in God's love?

 Write the first letters of their names on the flower.
Thank God for these helpers.

As Catholics...

We believe that God created angels. Angels are God's helpers. But they do not have bodies like people do. Angels give people messages from God. They protect and guide us. They never stop praising God.

How can you praise God, too?

25

God promises to love us always.

WE GATHER

✝ *God, we want to grow in your love forever.*

What does the word *forever* mean?

 Find another word for *forever*. Color the letters in the flowers.

ALWAYS

WE BELIEVE

God our Father loves us very much. He wants us to love him. In the Bible, there is a story about Adam and Eve.

📖 Genesis 2—3

Read Along

Adam and Eve lived in the most beautiful garden in the world. Everything was perfect there. God gave them everything they needed to live.

God wanted them to be happy with him forever.

One day Adam and Eve did something God had told them not to do. Then they had to live in a world that was not perfect any more.

26

God never stopped loving Adam and Eve.
He promised that he would be with
them always.
He promised to send someone to help
them and their children.

God our Father promises to be with
us and love us always, too.
He promises again and again to
save all people.

WE RESPOND

It is important for us
to remember God's promises.
What did God promise?

Put your right hand over
your heart.
Pray these words or use
your own words.
Thank you, God, for loving me always.
I promise to love you in return.

Circle the correct answer.

1. All things made by God are _____.

little   good

2. God created all _____ to know and love him.

people   animals

3. The Bible is a special _____ about God.

book   picture

4. God promises to love us _____.

only at special times   always

 **TALK ABOUT IT** How can people care for all God's creation?

 **ASSESSMENT** Make a sign to show some of God's gifts of creation. You might want to draw pictures on it or use pictures from magazines.

We Respond in Faith

Reflect & Pray

Draw or write to finish the prayer.
Dear God, I am happy in your wonderful world. I will show you I am happy by

Key Words

creation (p. 21)
Bible (p. 21)

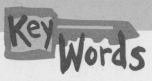

Remember

- God created the world.
- God created all people.
- God gives us special gifts.
- God promises to love us always.

OUR CATHOLIC LIFE

Saint Francis of Assisi

Saint Francis loved God and all of God's creation. He was kind and gentle to all God's creatures. He took care of God's world. Many Catholics follow his example. We celebrate the life of Saint Francis on October 4. On this day in some parishes, the priest blesses pets and other animals.

SHARING FAITH
with My Family

Sharing What I Learned

Look at the pictures below. Use each picture to tell your family what you learned in this chapter.

We Are Gifted

Choose a relative or friend of the family.
Together make a card to send to the person.
Have each member of your family write one
thing that they like about that person.
Then have everyone sign the card.
Send the card to your relative or friend.

You are a gift from God.
We are glad
that God created you.

Visit Sadlier's

www.WEBELIEVEweb.com

Connect to the Catechism
For adult background and reflection,
see paragraphs 344 and 337.

We Believe in the Blessed Trinity

2

✝ We Gather in Prayer

Let us stand to celebrate God's love.
For each action pray together,
"We thank you, God.
We celebrate your love."

Prayer Actions

- Raise your arms in the air.
- Clap your hands.
- Put your hands over your hearts.
- Close your eyes and bow your heads.

God sent his own Son, Jesus, to us.

WE GATHER

✝ *God, we celebrate your love for us.*

Have you ever waited for something
good to happen?
How did you feel while you
were waiting?

WE BELIEVE

People waited for God to keep
his promise to help us.
God the Father had a plan
for keeping his promise.
At a special time he sent his
own Son to us.

God sent Jesus to live with us
on earth.
God sent an angel to ask Mary
to be the mother of his own Son, Jesus.
Jesus showed us

- how much God loves us

- how to love God

- how to love ourselves

- how to love one another.

Jesus promised to help us, too!
He promised to send the Holy Spirit.
Jesus promised that the Holy Spirit
would always be our Helper.

WE RESPOND

Read each message. Color in the face
that shows how each message makes you feel.

- God loves you very much.

- God sent Jesus to us.

- Some people do keep promises.

- Some people do not keep promises.

What messages make you feel happy?

Pray:

God our Father, you kept your promise.
You sent your Son to help us.
Help us to keep the promises we make.

Jesus is God's greatest gift.

WE GATHER

✝ *God, thank you for sending Jesus to us.*

Name one gift you would like to receive on your birthday.

WE BELIEVE

God's greatest gift to us is Jesus. Jesus is the Son of God who became one of us. Jesus is our brother and our friend.

Jesus tells us about God's love. He tells us that God is our loving Father.

Jesus said, "As the Father loves me, so I also love you." (John 15:9)

We always have the gift of Jesus' love. Here is a story about his special love.

📖 Mark 10:13–14

Read Along

One day families came to Jesus with their children. They wanted Jesus to bless the children. Friends of Jesus told these people to go away. But Jesus said, "Let the children come to me." (Mark 10:14)

WE RESPOND

🧍 Why is Jesus God's greatest gift? Add yourself to the picture.

We believe that there are three Persons in one God.

WE GATHER

✝ *Jesus, thank you for showing us God's love.*

Join hands to make a circle.
Where is the end of the circle?
How can a circle remind us
about God's love?

WE BELIEVE

We believe that there is only one God.
We believe that there are three Persons
in one God.

Jesus taught us that
God the Father is God.
God the Son is God.
God the Holy Spirit is God.
The **Blessed Trinity** is one God in
three Persons.

- God the Father is the first Person
  of the Blessed Trinity.

- God the Son is the second Person
  of the Blessed Trinity.

- God the Holy Spirit is the third Person
  of the Blessed Trinity.

We believe that God the Father, God the Son,
and God the Holy Spirit are joined in love.

Key Word

Blessed Trinity one
God in three Persons:
God the Father,
God the Son, and
God the Holy Spirit

36

WE RESPOND

Sometimes pictures can help us to understand what we believe about the Blessed Trinity.

Look at the picture of the three circles joined together. Use one crayon to color the circles.

What can this picture help you to remember about the Blessed Trinity?

Pray:

God the Father, God the Son,
God the Holy Spirit,
we believe you are joined in love.

The Sign of the Cross is a prayer to the Blessed Trinity.

WE GATHER

✝ *God the Father, God the Son, and God the Holy Spirit, we praise you.*

What are these children doing? What do you think they are thinking or saying?

WE BELIEVE

When we pray, we show our love for God.
Prayer is listening to and talking to God.

Sometimes when we pray, we use special words from the Bible. Sometimes we use our own words. Sometimes we say prayers written by other people.

For some prayers we use actions as we pray.
The **Sign of the Cross** is a prayer to the Blessed Trinity:

In the name of the Father,
and of the Son,
and of the Holy Spirit.
Amen.

We begin our prayers by praying these words.

1. In the name of the Father,

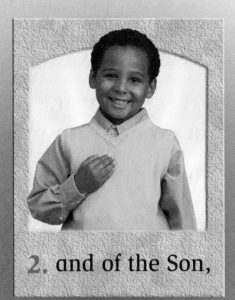

2. and of the Son,

3. and of the Holy

4. Spirit.

5. Amen.

WE RESPOND

Let us stand now and pray the Sign of the Cross.

The Sign of the Cross always reminds us that we believe in the Blessed Trinity.

Circle the correct answer.
Circle ? if you do not know the answer.

1. Jesus said the Holy Spirit would be
our Helper.

Yes   No   ?

2. God kept his promise by sending his
own Son, Jesus, to us.

Yes   No   ?

3. There is only one God.

Yes   No   ?

4. When we pray the Sign of the Cross,
we are praying only to God the Father.

Yes   No   ?

 Who are the three Persons of
the Blessed Trinity?

 Make your own copy of the three joined
circles on page 37. Add words to tell
what we believe about the Blessed Trinity.

We Respond in Faith

 **Reflect & Pray**

God, you always love me.
Your love makes me feel

 **Key Words**

Blessed Trinity (p. 36)
prayer (p. 39)
Sign of the Cross (p. 39)

Remember

- God sent his own Son, Jesus, to us.
- Jesus is God's greatest gift.
- We believe that there are three Persons in one God.
- The Sign of the Cross is a prayer to the Blessed Trinity.

OUR CATHOLIC LIFE

The Sign of the Cross at Mass

Catholics all over the world come together at Mass to pray to God. We all begin the Mass by making the sign of the cross. This shows that we believe in God the Father, God the Son, and God the Holy Spirit.

SHARING FAITH
with My Family

Sharing What I Learned

Look at the pictures below. Use each picture to tell your family what you learned in this chapter.

For All to See and Pray

Pray the Sign of the Cross often with your family.

1 In the name of the Father,

2 and of the Son,

3 and of the Holy

4 Spirit.

5 Amen.

Visit Sadlier's

www.WeBelieveweb.com

Connect to the Catechism
For adult background and reflection, see paragraphs 422, 423, 234, and 232.

Jesus Grew Up in a Family

✝ We Gather in Prayer

Leader: Let us stand and pray together. For our families, that we may all keep growing in God's love, we pray,

All: God, please help us to share your love.

Leader: For families who are going to welcome new babies soon, we pray,

All: God, please help them to grow in your love.

Leader: For families who do not have everything they need to live, we pray,

All: God, please help us to take care of them.

God chose Mary to be the mother of his Son.

WE GATHER

✝ *God, we need your love and your care.*

🧍 Look at each picture.
If it shows people today, circle NOW.
If it shows people in the time of Jesus, circle THEN.

NOW

THEN

NOW

THEN

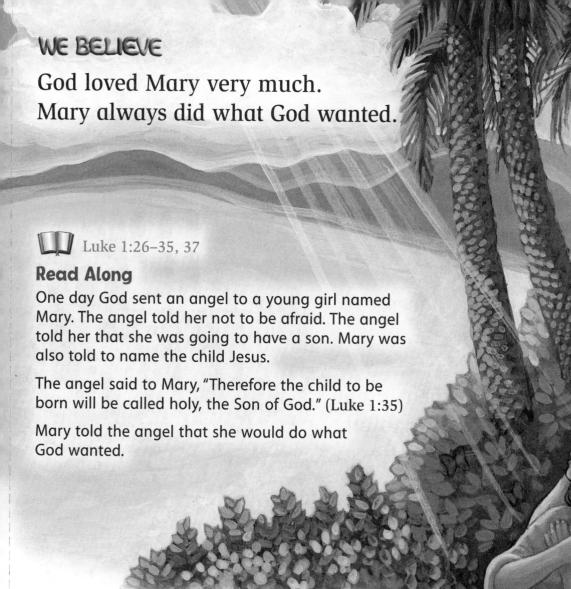

WE BELIEVE

God loved Mary very much.
Mary always did what God wanted.

📖 Luke 1:26–35, 37

Read Along

One day God sent an angel to a young girl named Mary. The angel told her not to be afraid. The angel told her that she was going to have a son. Mary was also told to name the child Jesus.

The angel said to Mary, "Therefore the child to be born will be called holy, the Son of God." (Luke 1:35)

Mary told the angel that she would do what God wanted.

Mary is the mother of God's only Son, Jesus.
Jesus loves his mother.
He wants us to love her, too.

WE RESPOND

Mary did what God asked of her.
We can, too.
What is one thing God asks you to do today?

Ask Mary for help. Pray together:
Holy Mary, Mother of God, pray for us.

45

Jesus was born in Bethlehem.

WE GATHER

✝ *God our Father, thank you for Jesus, your Son.*

Where do you live?
Have you lived in other places?

WE BELIEVE

Mary married a man named Joseph.
They lived in the town of Nazareth.
Mary was going to have a baby.
Mary and Joseph were waiting
for Jesus to be born.

 Luke 2:1–7

Read Along

During that time a new rule was made. All men had to go back to the town of their father's family. They had to sign a list and be counted.

Joseph was from the town of Bethlehem.
So he and Mary had to go there.

When Mary and Joseph got to Bethlehem, it was very crowded. They looked for a place to stay. There was no room for them anywhere. At last, they found a place where animals were kept. They rested there. Later that night, Mary had a baby boy.

"She wrapped him in swaddling clothes and laid him in a manger, because there was no room for them in the inn." (Luke 2:7)

God the Father loved us so much. He sent his Son into the world. At **Christmas** we celebrate the birth of Jesus.

One way we celebrate is by sharing the story of what happened when Jesus was born.

WE RESPOND

What would you tell your family and friends about the birth of Jesus?

Christmas the time when we celebrate the birth of Jesus

Diego Rivera, artist
"Las Posadas"

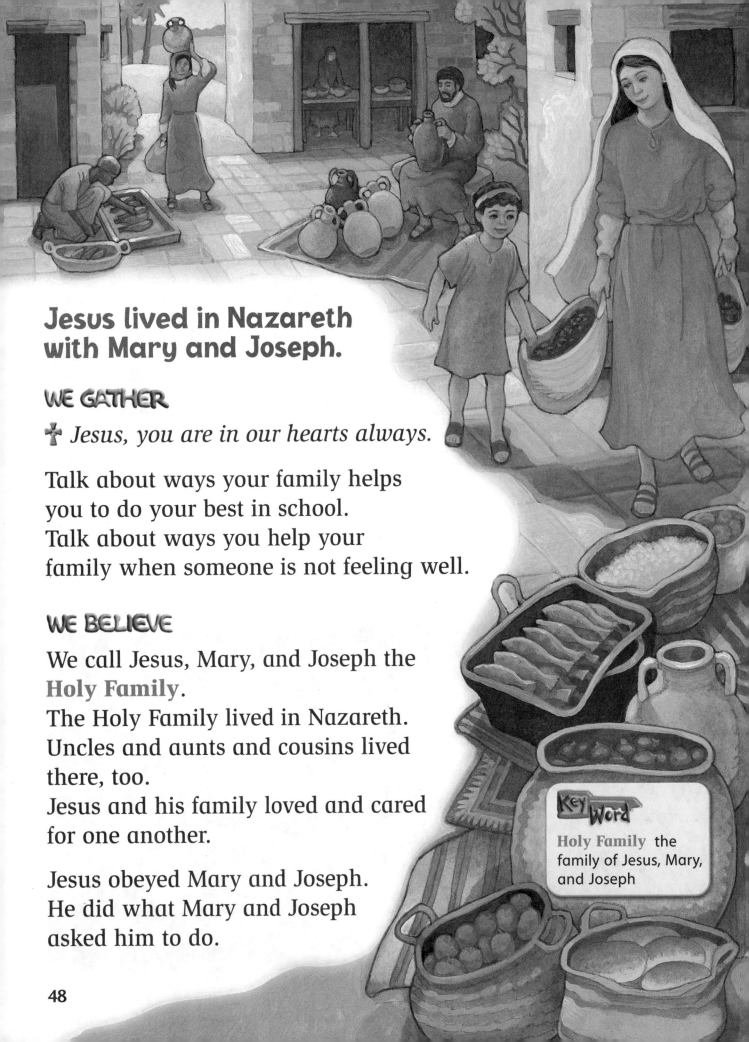

Jesus lived in Nazareth with Mary and Joseph.

WE GATHER

✝ *Jesus, you are in our hearts always.*

Talk about ways your family helps you to do your best in school.
Talk about ways you help your family when someone is not feeling well.

WE BELIEVE

We call Jesus, Mary, and Joseph the **Holy Family**.
The Holy Family lived in Nazareth. Uncles and aunts and cousins lived there, too.
Jesus and his family loved and cared for one another.

Jesus obeyed Mary and Joseph. He did what Mary and Joseph asked him to do.

Key Word

Holy Family the family of Jesus, Mary, and Joseph

WE RESPOND

Think about ways Jesus, Mary, and Joseph helped one another. What are ways you will help your family?

 Read the following sentences. Color the heart only if it is next to a way you can help your family.

♡ Take turns choosing TV programs.

♡ Make fun of people.

♡ Play fair.

♡ Obey my parents or those who care for me.

♡ Be mean to my brothers, sisters, or friends.

Pray quietly.

Jesus, help me to be like you. I want to help my family, too.

The Holy Family obeyed God the Father and prayed to him.

WE GATHER

✝ *Jesus, Mary, and Joseph, please help our families to love God.*

 Imagine that the Holy Family is coming to visit. Draw a picture to show your family getting ready.

WE BELIEVE

Jesus, Mary, and Joseph believed
in the one, true God.
They loved God very much.
They obeyed God's laws.
They helped each other at home.
They helped other people.
They obeyed the laws of their country.

The Holy Family prayed to God.
They prayed every morning and
every night.
They joined other Jewish families
for prayer each week.
They listened to stories about
God and his people.

WE RESPOND

When does your family pray together?
Share this prayer at your family meals.

Bless us, O Lord,
and these your gifts
which we are about to
receive from your goodness.
Through Christ our Lord.
Amen.

Review

Circle the correct answer.

1. Jesus was born in _____.

Bethlehem   Nazareth

2. When Jesus was growing up, the Holy Family lived in _____.

Bethlehem   Nazareth

3. We celebrate the birth of Jesus on _____.

Christmas   Easter

4. Mary _____ did what God asked her to do.

always   never

 **TALK ABOUT IT** Who are the members of the Holy Family?

 **ASSESSMENT** Make a booklet. Show the ways the Holy Family loved each other and showed their love for God.

We Respond in Faith

Reflect & Pray

Holy Family, I

Key Words

Christmas (p. 47)
Holy Family (p. 48)

Remember

- God chose Mary to be the mother of his Son.
- Jesus was born in Bethlehem.
- Jesus lived in Nazareth with Mary and Joseph.
- The Holy Family obeyed God the Father and prayed to him.

OUR CATHOLIC LIFE

Feast of the Holy Family

Every year Catholics honor the Holy Family on the first Sunday after Christmas. On this day, we praise God together with other families. We ask Jesus, Mary, and Joseph to help our families. We ask God the Father to help us to be more like the Holy Family.

SHARING FAITH
with My Family

Sharing What I Learned

Look at the pictures below. Use each picture to tell your family what you learned in this chapter.

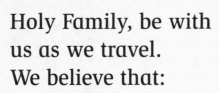

Family Travels

Many times the Holy Family traveled together.
Put this prayer card in a convenient place.
Say the prayer together when you begin your trips.

Holy Family, be with
us as we travel.
We believe that:

- all God's ways are
  beautiful.

- all his paths lead
  us to peace and
  happiness.

Visit Sadlier's

www.WeBelieveweb.com

Connect to the Catechism
For adult background and reflection,
see paragraphs 484, 525, 531, and 532.

Jesus Works Among the People

4

✝ We Gather in Prayer

🎵 Jesus in the Morning

Jesus, Jesus,
Jesus in the morning,
Jesus at the noontime;
Jesus, Jesus,
Jesus when the sun goes down!

Love him, love him,
Love him in the morning,
Love him at the noontime;
Love him, love him,
Love him when the sun goes down!

John the Baptist helped people to get ready for Jesus.

WE GATHER

✝ *Jesus, be with us always.*

Have you ever helped get ready to
welcome a special visitor at home?
At school?
What did you do to help?

WE BELIEVE

John was the cousin of Jesus.
When John grew up, he went to live
in the desert.
He became one of God's helpers.

God gave John an important message
to share.
John told people to put God first
in their lives.
John told them not to be selfish.
He told them to share and be fair.

Many people heard John's message. John, called John the Baptist, was getting the people ready. They were getting ready to welcome Jesus, the Son of God, into their lives. Jesus would show them the way God wanted them to live.

WE RESPOND

You need to be ready to welcome Jesus every day.

Circle one way you can welcome Jesus.

Share with my friends.

Say my prayers.

Be fair when I play.

Say "please" and "thank you."

Help my family at home.

What other ways can you welcome Jesus?

Jesus shared God's love with all people.

WE GATHER

✝ *Jesus, welcome into our lives.*

Think about the people you see
in your town.
What are they like? What do they do?

WE BELIEVE

When Jesus was a grown-up, he left
his home in Nazareth.
He went from town to town
teaching people.
He told them about God and his
great love.

Jesus treated all people with respect.
He shared the news of God's love
with everyone. He shared with

- children and parents
- farmers and fishermen
- poor people and rich people
- those who were sick and those
  who were healthy.

Here is a story about someone Jesus met.

📖 Luke 19:1–5

Read Along

One day Jesus visited a town called Jericho. A large crowd gathered to see Jesus. A very rich man named Zacchaeus wanted to see Jesus, too. Zacchaeus was so short that he could not see above the heads of the other people. He climbed a tree and sat in the branches so that he could see Jesus.

When Jesus came to the tree, he looked up. He said, "Zacchaeus, come down quickly, for today I must stay at your house." (Luke 19:5)

Zacchaeus was very happy. Jesus was coming to his house. Jesus knew that Zacchaeus needed to hear the news of God's love, too.

WE RESPOND

🧍 Act out the story of Zacchaeus. What did you learn about Jesus from this story?

Thank Jesus for sharing God's great love.

Jesus teaches that God watches over us and cares for us.

WE GATHER

✝ *God, we need your love always.*

What are some things that are important to you?
Show how you take care of one of them.

WE BELIEVE

Jesus wanted people to know about God.
He wanted everyone to know that
God takes care of them.

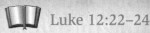 Luke 12:22–24

Read Along

One day Jesus was teaching. He pointed to the birds flying above the crowd. Jesus said that the birds did not have to worry about food. God cares for the birds. Jesus told the crowd that God cares for people even more! He said, "How much more important are you than birds!" (Luke 12:24)

Do you know how important we are to God?
God watches over us all the time.
He loves and takes care of us even when we do not know it.
When we believe someone loves us, we **trust** them.
Jesus tells us to trust God.

WE RESPOND

How does God watch over you?

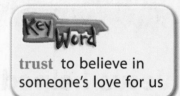

♪ People Worry

People worry about this and that.
People worry about this and that!
But Jesus tells us, "Don't worry.
Don't worry about this and that!"

God knows ev'rything we need,
  just believe, just believe.
God takes care of ev'ryone.
Trust in God, trust in God.

As Catholics...

We all need to take quiet time to pray to God. We can praise God. We can thank God. We can ask God for help. Before Jesus began to teach, he went into the desert. He went there to pray to God.

Where is your special place to pray?

Jesus helped all those in need.

WE GATHER

✝ *Jesus, thank you for teaching that God cares for us.*

How do you know that someone loves and cares for you?
What does the person say?
What does the person do?

WE BELIEVE

Jesus cared for all people.
He welcomed and blessed the children.
He comforted people who were sad
or afraid.

Jesus helped the poor.
He fed the hungry.
He healed many people who were sick.
He loved everyone, even those who did
not like him.

📖 Matthew 20:29–33

Read Along

One day a large crowd was following Jesus. Two blind men heard that Jesus was passing by. They cried out to him for help. Jesus stopped and asked, "What do you want me to do for you?" They answered him, "Lord, let our eyes be opened." (Matthew 20:32–33)

Then Jesus touched their eyes. Right away the two men could see. They began to follow Jesus.

WE RESPOND

What do you think the two men said after Jesus healed them?

 Finish this prayer. Match each picture to the right words.

Jesus,

- Open my ___s. May they *see* people who need help.

- Help my ___s to *hear* your word.

- Let my ___s *do* good for others.

63

Circle the correct answer.
Circle ? if you do not know the answer.

1. Zacchaeus was the cousin of Jesus.

Yes   No   ?

2. To trust God means to believe in his love for us.

Yes   No   ?

3. Jesus treated all people with respect.

Yes   No   ?

4. Jesus showed God's love by healing the sick.

Yes   No   ?

 **TALK ABOUT IT** Who was John the Baptist?

 **ASSESSMENT** Tell some of the ways Jesus showed people God's love. Draw a picture of Jesus doing one of these things.

We Respond in Faith

Reflect & Pray

Jesus, thank you for all those who help me learn more about you. Thank you for

Key Word

trust (p. 61)

Remember

- John the Baptist helped people to get ready for Jesus.
- Jesus shared God's love with all people.
- Jesus teaches that God watches over us and cares for us.
- Jesus helped all those in need.

OUR CATHOLIC LIFE

Care for the Sick

In many hospitals there are people who help the patients and their families. These people help the patients by:
- praying with them
- cheering them up
- listening to their problems
- reading stories from the Bible
- bringing Holy Communion to them.

Think of something you and your family can do for people who are sick.

SHARING FAITH
with My Family

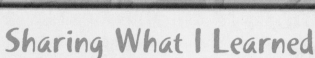

Sharing What I Learned

Look at the pictures below. Use each picture to tell your family what you learned in this chapter.

Loving Others Day by Day

Put a weekly calendar on your refrigerator door. Each day, have the members of your family write how they showed love that day. Then read about the love your family shared!

Sunday
Monday
Tuesday
Wednesday
Thursday
Friday
Saturday

Visit Sadlier's

www.WeBelieveweb.com

Connect to the Catechism
For adult background and reflection, see paragraphs 535, 542, 305, and 544.

Jesus Teaches Us About Love

5

✝ We Gather in Prayer

Leader: • Jesus, you blessed the children who came to see you. We ask you to bless us now.

All: • Jesus, bless our eyes so we may see your love.

• Jesus, bless our ears so we may hear your words of love.

• Jesus, bless our hands so we may share your love.

• Jesus, bless our mouths so we may tell others about your love.

• Jesus, fill our hearts with love.

Many people wanted to follow Jesus.

WE GATHER

✝ *Jesus, bless us.*

Think about the people you know.
Who do you like to spend time with?
Why?

WE BELIEVE

Jesus traveled from place to place.
News about him spread everywhere.
Many people went looking for Jesus.

When Jesus taught, crowds of people
would come to hear him.
One day Jesus even had to get on a boat
so all the people could see and hear him.

Why did crowds of people come to Jesus?
The people needed him to:

- make them feel better

- teach them to pray

- tell them the good news
  about God's love

- tell them how to live a better life.

After spending time with Jesus, people came to know what God's love was like.
Jesus made everyone feel special.

WE RESPOND

How can you spend time with Jesus?

Circle each thing you can do.

- Pray.

- Listen to a story about Jesus.

- Share Jesus' love with others.

69

Jesus taught the Great Commandment.

WE GATHER

✝ *Jesus, we want to follow you.*

What is one of your family's rules? How does keeping this rule help you and your family?

WE BELIEVE

Commandments are laws or rules given to us by God. These laws help us to live as God wants us to.

Jesus taught us the Great Commandment. He said,

"You shall love the Lord, your God, with all your heart, with all your soul, and with all your mind.
You shall love your neighbor as yourself."

(Matthew 22:37, 39)

When we follow this commandment,
we do what God wants us to do.
We love God, ourselves, and others.

We show God our love in these ways.

- We do what God wants us to do.
- We go to Mass on Sunday.
- We pray to God everyday.
- We make the sign of the cross with respect.

Key Word

commandments
laws or rules given to us by God

WE RESPOND

What are other ways you can show your love for God?

Pray these words.
My God, I offer you today all
I think and do and say.

As Catholics...

When we wake up in the morning, we can pray to God. This shows how important God is to us. There are special prayers we say to offer God our whole day. We call these prayers morning offerings. You can say the prayer on this page as a morning offering.

Jesus taught us to love God, ourselves, and others.

WE GATHER

✝ *God the Father, God the Son, and God the Holy Spirit, help us.*

You show love for yourself when you eat the right foods.
What other things can you do to show that you love yourself?

WE BELIEVE

When we learn about Jesus' teaching, we learn about love.
God made us to show us his love.
We show God we love ourselves when we take care of ourselves.
We can share our love with others, too.

Jesus showed us how to love people.
He was kind.
He listened to people's problems.
He cared for all people.
Jesus wants us to act as he acted.
We do this when we love God, ourselves, and others.

WE RESPOND

Say a prayer to Jesus. Ask Jesus to help you to love others as he did.

Look at the pictures. Color the star beside the pictures that show people acting as Jesus did.

Jesus taught us that all people are our neighbors.

WE GATHER

✝ *Jesus, help us to love others as you did.*

Who are your neighbors? How do you help them?

WE BELIEVE

After Jesus taught the Great Commandment, someone asked who our neighbors are. Jesus answered by telling this story.

 Luke 10:30–35

Read Along

One day a man was walking down the road. Robbers hurt him and took his money. They left the man on the side of the road.

A priest walked by the person who was hurt. He did not stop to help. Then another religious leader passed and saw the hurt man. But he kept walking. Finally, a man from the country called Samaria stopped to help him. He rubbed oil on the man's cuts and covered them with bandages. The Samaritan brought the hurt man to a roadside inn.

The next day the Samaritan had to leave. He said to the innkeeper, "Take care of him. If you spend more than I have given you, I shall repay you on my way back." (Luke 10:35)

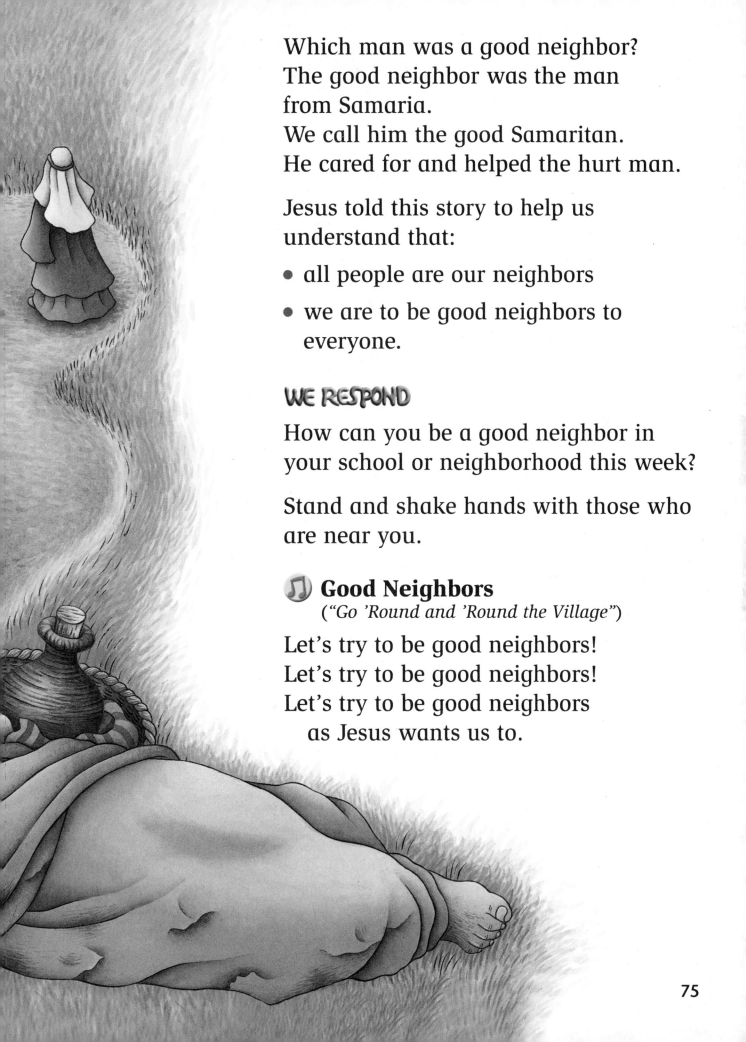

Which man was a good neighbor?
The good neighbor was the man
from Samaria.
We call him the good Samaritan.
He cared for and helped the hurt man.

Jesus told this story to help us
understand that:

- all people are our neighbors

- we are to be good neighbors to
  everyone.

WE RESPOND

How can you be a good neighbor in
your school or neighborhood this week?

Stand and shake hands with those who
are near you.

Good Neighbors
("Go 'Round and 'Round the Village")

Let's try to be good neighbors!
Let's try to be good neighbors!
Let's try to be good neighbors
   as Jesus wants us to.

Circle the correct answer.

1. Jesus taught us that _____ people are our neighbors.

    all   some

2. _____ people came to hear Jesus.

    Many   Few

3. We show God our love when we _____.

    hurt others   love ourselves

4. Commandments are _____ given to us by God.

    laws   tests

 What did Jesus teach us in the story of the good Samaritan?

 Draw pictures of or write about
- ways we show our love for God
- ways we show our love for others.

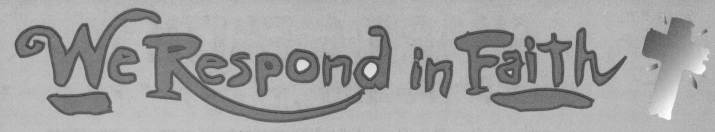

We Respond in Faith

 Reflect & Pray

Finish the prayer. Trace over the last two words.

Jesus, help me to be a
_____

 good neighbor.

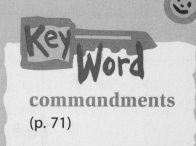

Key Word

commandments
(p. 71)

Remember

• Many people wanted to follow Jesus.

• Jesus taught the Great Commandment.

• Jesus taught us to love God, ourselves, and others.

• Jesus taught us that all people are our neighbors.

OUR CATHOLIC LIFE

Our Human Family

Jesus taught us that we are all members of one human family. We are all neighbors. Here are some ways you can show love for your neighbors. Be kind at home, at school, and in your neighborhood. With your family learn more about people who are living in different neighborhoods or in other countries.

SHARING FAITH
with My Family

Sharing What I Learned

Look at the pictures below. Use each picture to tell your family what you learned in this chapter.

Good Neighbors

Talk together about ways family members can be good neighbors this week. Choose one or two of these ways. Write them below.

Visit Sadlier's

www.WE BELIEVE web.com

 Connect to the Catechism
For adult background and reflection, see paragraphs 544–546, 2055, and 1931.

The Church Year

Praise to you, Lord Jesus Christ.

The Church praises Jesus all year long.

WE GATHER

What does the word *praise* mean to you?

WE BELIEVE

All year long the Church gathers to thank God for his great love. Together, we praise God. We celebrate all that Jesus did for us.

Advent

Christmas

Ordinary Time

Ordinary Time

Lent

Three Days

Easter

Every year we have special times to praise and thank God. Each year we join together to celebrate these special times.

Read Along

Advent is a time of waiting. We wait and get ready for the coming of the Son of God.

Christmas is a time to celebrate the birth of the Son of God. We celebrate God's greatest gift to us, his Son, Jesus.

Lent is a time to remember all that Jesus has done for us. We get ready for the Church's great celebration.

The Three Days are the Church's greatest celebration. We remember and celebrate that Jesus died for us and rose to new life.

Easter is a time of great joy. We rejoice and celebrate that Jesus rose to new life.

Ordinary Time is when we celebrate everything about Jesus, especially his life and teachings.

The Church year helps us to follow Jesus. The different times help us remember and celebrate all that Jesus did for us. The times also help us remember that Jesus is with us today!

All during the year we thank Jesus for the gift of himself. We thank him for being with us always.

WE RESPOND

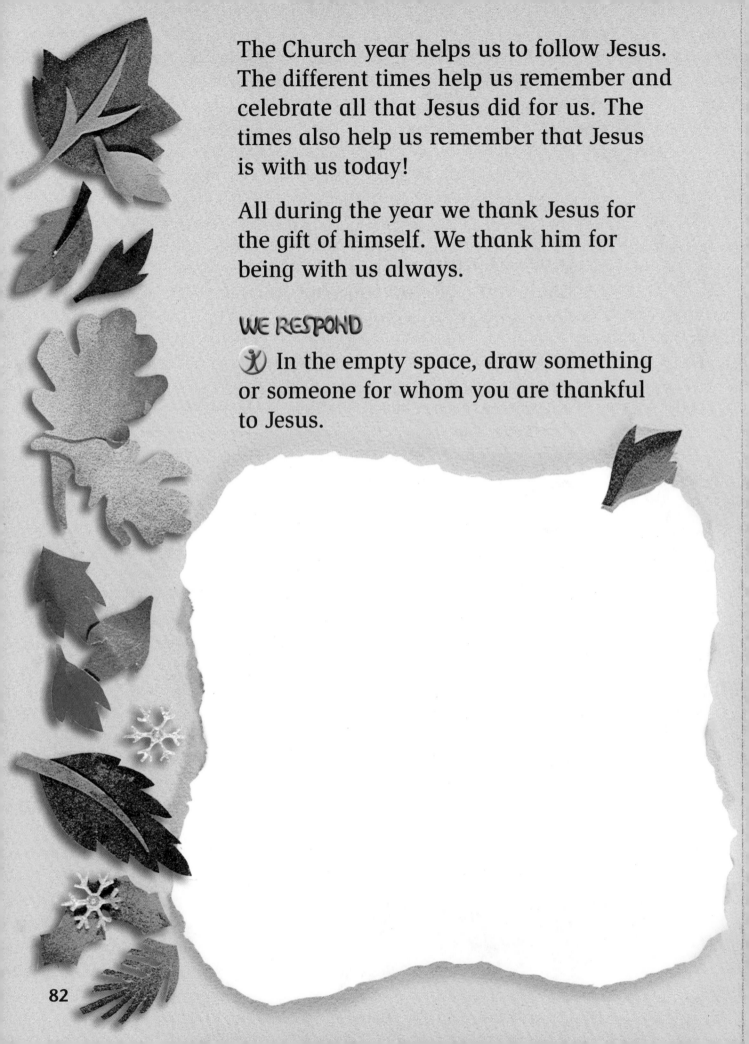 In the empty space, draw something or someone for whom you are thankful to Jesus.

✝ We Respond in Prayer

Leader: During the Church year we celebrate that Jesus is with us all the time.

Leader: We pray in Advent:

All: Come, Lord Jesus!

Leader: We pray during Christmas:

All: Rejoice! Jesus is born!

Leader: We pray in Lent:

All: Lord, have mercy.

Leader: We pray during the Three Days:

All: Jesus, bring us new life.

Leader: We pray during Easter:

All: Alleluia! Christ is risen!

Leader: We pray in Ordinary Time:

All: Praised be the name of Jesus!

Leader: We remember that Jesus is with us each and every day of the year.

All: Praised be the name of Jesus!

SHARING FAITH
with My Family

Sharing What I Learned

Look at the pictures below. Use them to tell your family what you learned in this chapter.

A Family Prayer of Praise and Thanks

We praise you, Lord,
All through the year,
As seasons come and go.

We praise you, Lord,
For you are here
And with us now, we know.

Give praise and thanks to the Father!
Give praise and thanks to Jesus, his Son!
Give praise and thanks to the Holy Spirit!
Amen! Amen! Amen!

Visit Sadlier's

www.WeBelieveweb.com

 Connect to the Catechism
For adult background and reflection,
see paragraph 1168.

Ordinary Time

Advent | Christmas | Ordinary Time | Lent | Three Days | Easter | Ordinary Time

Give thanks to the Lord,
his love is everlasting.

85

The Church celebrates the life and teachings of Jesus.

WE GATHER

We can put things in order by numbering them.

What is the biggest number of things that you have put in order?

WE BELIEVE

The Church has special times to celebrate. During Ordinary Time, we celebrate the life and teachings of Jesus. We try to follow him more closely each day. This season is called Ordinary Time because the Church puts the Sundays in number *order*.

Every Sunday of the year is a special day. Every Sunday we celebrate the Mass. We remember the things Jesus has done for us. We thank Jesus for the gift of himself.

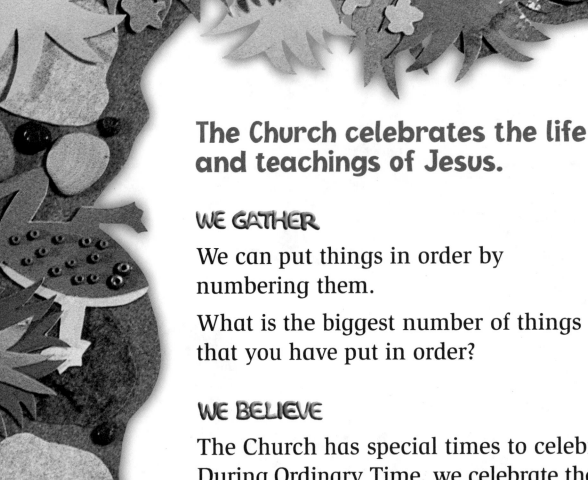

We hear wonderful stories about

- Jesus' teaching, healing, and forgiving

- the first followers of Jesus

- the Holy Spirit helping the first members of the Church.

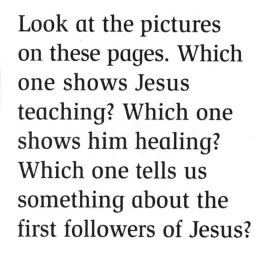

Look at the pictures on these pages. Which one shows Jesus teaching? Which one shows him healing? Which one tells us something about the first followers of Jesus?

Share your answers.

Saints are followers of Jesus who loved him very much. The saints have died, but they now live forever with God. The lives of the saints show us how to be followers of Jesus.

We celebrate many special days during Ordinary Time. One of them is called All Saints' Day. It is celebrated on November 1.

WE RESPOND

Draw yourself here. Write one way you are a follower of Jesus.

✝ We Respond in Prayer

Leader: We are all children of God. On All Saints' Day, we celebrate all the children of God who are living forever with God. They are called saints.

Reader: Let us listen to the word of God.

"Blessed are the peacemakers, for they will be called children of God." (Matthew 5:9)

The Gospel of the Lord.

All: Praise to you, Lord Jesus Christ.

Leader: The saints are children of God. We honor them because they loved God and loved others. We are children of God. We can love God and love others, too!

🎵 Children of God

Children of God is what we are.
Children of God we all must be.
Children of God; that's you and me.
Thanks be to God.
Thanks be to God.
We all stand in need to be thankful
for making us children of God.

Sharing What I Learned

Look at the pictures below. Use them to tell your family what you learned in this chapter.

Around the Table

On Sundays in Ordinary Time, we hear the teachings of Jesus. After Mass this Sunday, talk about the gospel reading that you listened to. What does Jesus teach us? How does he want us to live?

As a family decorate the words below. Together ask Jesus to help you put them into action.

LOVE ONE ANOTHER
AS I LOVE YOU.

John 15:12

Visit Sadlier's

www.WeBelieve.web.com

Connect to the Catechism
For adult background and reflection, see paragraph 1163.

Grade 1
Unit 1

Circle the correct answer.

1. The Bible is a special book about _____.

    God   trees

2. God sent his own Son, _____, to us.

    Joseph   Jesus

3. On Christmas, we celebrate the birth of _____.

    Jesus   Mary

4. Jesus was mean to many people.

    Yes   No

5. God created our world.

    Yes   No

6. Jesus teaches that God watches over us and cares for us.

    Yes   No

 What is the Great Commandment? How can we follow the Great Commandment?

91

Draw a picture.
Show Jesus with his family.
Tell what you know about Jesus' family.

Look at the two pictures below.
For each picture, tell what Jesus is
doing and saying.

We Are Followers of Jesus

UNIT 2 SHARING FAITH as a Family

Five Essentials of Family Prayer

Prayer is an indispensable part of the spiritual life. With today's hectic schedules, praying together as a family may seem unattainable. This doesn't have to be the case, especially when keeping some essential practices in mind:

1. *Keep it simple.* Jesus' instructions were very basic: go to your room and pray! Family prayer works the same way. We go to a room, or special place, and pray. Together, we speak and listen to God.

2. *Pray often.* No place is inappropriate for prayer. Families on the move can share blessings in the car or on the way out the door. We can pray at different times of the day and in all the seasons of our lives.

3. *Use different types of prayer.* The Church has used various forms of prayer throughout the centuries—praise, thanksgiving, intercession, blessing, and petition. Drawing upon the treasured resources of the Church keeps family prayer alive, dynamic, and intriguing.

4. *Vary configurations.* Waiting for the entire family to assemble in one place for prayer could take months! Praying in smaller groups, such as parent with child, husband with wife, etc., still constitutes family devotion. It also keeps family prayer alive.

5. *Build community.* Prayer thrives in families that remain close, and families grow closer by praying together!

From the Catechism

"Parents' respect and affection are expressed by the care and attention they devote to bringing up their young children and *providing for their physical and spiritual needs.*"
(Catechism of the Catholic Church, 2228)

What Your Child Will Learn in Unit 2

Unit 2 introduces the children to a history of the Church that culminates with how the Church cares for us today. The children will learn that Jesus attracted many followers. Jesus taught his followers many things. One teaching concerned how we are to pray. The meaning of the Lord's Prayer is explained to the children. Continuing the story of the Church, Unit 2 presents Jesus as the Good Shepherd. The events surrounding Jesus' death and Resurrection are presented in ways that first graders can handle. The coming of the Holy Spirit at Pentecost begins the history of the Church. The children will understand that the Holy Spirit helped the Church to grow in its early days and continues to help the Church today through the leadership of the pope and the bishops.

Plan & Preview

▶ Set up a prayer table in a prominent place in your home. You might include a family Bible, pictures of Jesus and Mary, some unlit candles, perhaps a growing plant of some kind, etc. *(Chapter 9 Family Page)*

▶ You might want to have some sheets of tracing paper or light paper. *(Chapter 10 Family Page)*

Thank You, God

A Caregiver's Meditation

Select a time when you make sure you have a few moments to yourself. If possible, darken the room, play some soothing background music. Count backwards 20 to 1, inhaling and then exhaling on each count. As you do so, also concentrate on the word, *Jesus.* Feel his presence with you. Rest quietly. Now count 1 to 5 as you raise yourself up to face the challenges of the day.

Bible Q & A

Q: How can I use the Bible to talk to my daughter about the Pentecost story?
—Reno, Nevada

A: Read Acts of the Apostles 2:1–13. Ask your daughter to draw a picture of the Pentecost event.

Jesus Had Many Followers

8

✝ **We Gather in Prayer**

🎵 **Jesus Wants to Help Us**

We believe Jesus wants to help us.
We believe Jesus wants to help us.
We believe that Jesus
   always wants to help us.

When we pray, Jesus wants to hear us.
When we pray, Jesus wants to hear us.
We believe that Jesus
   always wants to hear us.

Jesus invited people to be his followers.

WE GATHER

✝ *Jesus, please help us to be your followers.*

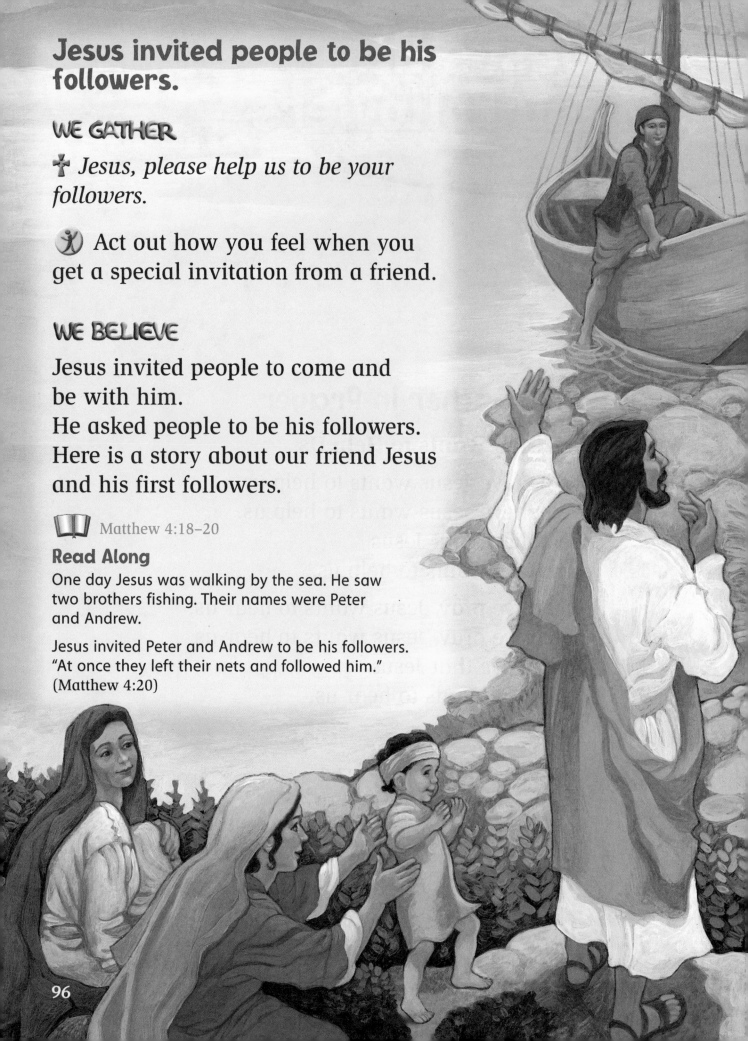 Act out how you feel when you get a special invitation from a friend.

WE BELIEVE

Jesus invited people to come and be with him.
He asked people to be his followers.
Here is a story about our friend Jesus and his first followers.

📖 Matthew 4:18–20

Read Along

One day Jesus was walking by the sea. He saw two brothers fishing. Their names were Peter and Andrew.

Jesus invited Peter and Andrew to be his followers. "At once they left their nets and followed him." (Matthew 4:20)

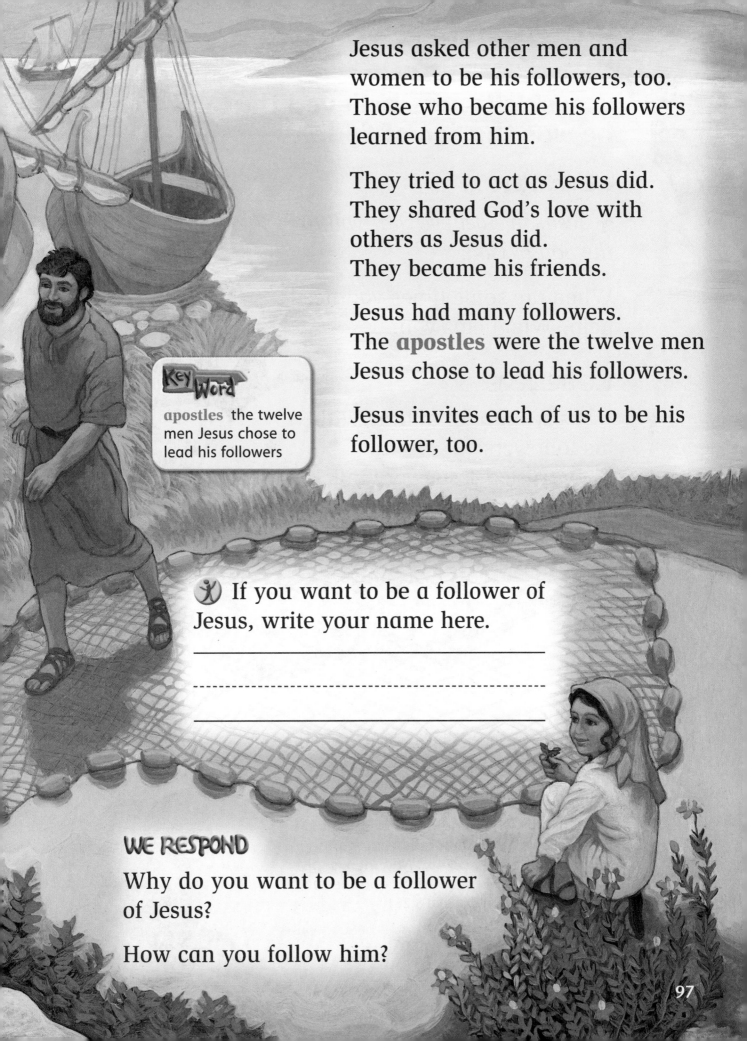

Jesus asked other men and women to be his followers, too. Those who became his followers learned from him.

They tried to act as Jesus did. They shared God's love with others as Jesus did. They became his friends.

Jesus had many followers. The **apostles** were the twelve men Jesus chose to lead his followers.

Jesus invites each of us to be his follower, too.

Key Word

apostles the twelve men Jesus chose to lead his followers

If you want to be a follower of Jesus, write your name here.

_____

- -

_____

WE RESPOND

Why do you want to be a follower of Jesus?

How can you follow him?

Jesus' followers believed that he was the Son of God.

WE GATHER

✝ *Jesus, we believe that you are the Son of God.*

When are some times you need help? Who helps you?

WE BELIEVE

Jesus spent a lot of time with his followers.
They trusted Jesus very much.
Here is a story about a time when Jesus helped his followers.

📖 Luke 8:22–25

Read Along

One day Jesus was in a boat with his followers. He fell asleep. Soon a storm started rocking the boat. Jesus' followers were afraid. They woke Jesus up. They believed he would help them.

Jesus told the winds and waves to be still. Jesus' followers were amazed because the storm stopped. They asked, "Who then is this, who commands even the winds and the sea, and they obey him?" (Luke 8:25)

🏃 Act out the story.

Jesus did amazing things to
help people.
Jesus calmed the storm.
He did many things that only God
can do.
Jesus' followers saw these things and
believed in him.
They believed Jesus was the Son of God.

WE RESPOND

Imagine that you were on that boat
with Jesus.
What would you have said to Jesus
after he calmed the storm?

What will you do to show that you
believe in Jesus?

Pray together.
Jesus, Son of God, we believe in you.

Jesus showed his followers how to pray.

WE GATHER

✝ *Jesus, you are always with us.*

Talk about something you have learned by listening to others.

Talk about something you have learned by watching other people.

WE BELIEVE

Jesus often prayed to God the Father. Sometimes Jesus prayed alone. Sometimes he prayed with other people.

Jesus' followers learned to pray by watching him pray.
They learned to pray by listening to Jesus, too.

 Luke 11:1–2

Read Along

One day Jesus was praying. When he was finished, one of his followers asked him to teach the group to pray.

Jesus told his followers, "When you pray, say: 'Father, hallowed be your name.'" (Luke 11:2)

We call the prayer Jesus taught his followers the **Lord's Prayer**.
We also call this prayer the Our Father.
Here are the words we pray.

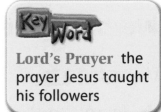

Lord's Prayer the prayer Jesus taught his followers

Our Father, who art in heaven,
hallowed be thy name;
thy kingdom come;
thy will be done on earth as it is in
  heaven.
Give us this day our daily bread;
and forgive us our trespasses
as we forgive those who trespass
  against us;
and lead us not into temptation,
but deliver us from evil.
Amen.

Decorate the prayer frame.

As Catholics...

Lord is another name for God. Jesus' followers sometimes called him Lord. We use the name *Lord* in many of our prayers. When we do this, we remember that Jesus is the Son of God.

During Sunday Mass, listen for the times we pray, "Lord."

WE RESPOND

Who teaches you to pray?
Why do you pray?

We pray the Lord's Prayer.

WE GATHER

✝ *Jesus, teach us to pray as you did.*

 Draw a picture to show a time you prayed with your family.

WE BELIEVE

Jesus taught his followers the Lord's Prayer.

We can pray this prayer with others or by ourselves.

The Lord's Prayer	When we pray this prayer:
Our Father, who art in heaven,	We praise God. We pray to God as our loving Father.
hallowed be thy name;	We say that God is holy. We honor and respect his name.
thy kingdom come; thy will be done on earth as it is in heaven.	We ask that all people will know and share God's love. This is what God wants for all of us.
Give us this day our daily bread;	We ask God to give us what we need. We remember all people who are hungry or poor.
and forgive us our trespasses as we forgive those who trespass against us;	We ask God to forgive us. We need to forgive others.
and lead us not into temptation, but deliver us from evil. Amen.	We ask God to keep us free from anything that goes against his love.

 Make up actions for the Lord's Prayer.

WE RESPOND

When do you hear the Lord's Prayer prayed?

Gather in a circle. Pray the Lord's Prayer together.

Circle the correct answer.

1. The _____ of Jesus learned from him.

   teachers   followers

2. Jesus' followers believed that he was _____.

   the Son of God   an apostle

3. Jesus taught his followers the _____.

   Sign of the Cross   Lord's Prayer

4. The _____ men Jesus chose to lead his followers were the apostles.

   twelve   ten

 **TALK ABOUT IT** Why is the Lord's Prayer a special prayer?

 **ASSESSMENT** Write sentences or draw pictures about Jesus' first followers. What did they see? What did they hear?

We Respond in Faith

Reflect & Pray

Jesus, I want to be your friend and follower. I can

Remember

- Jesus invited people to be his followers.
- Jesus' followers believed that he was the Son of God.
- Jesus showed his followers how to pray.
- We pray the Lord's Prayer.

OUR CATHOLIC LIFE

Our Daily Bread

"Give us this day our daily bread." When we pray these words from the Lord's Prayer, we are praying for the needs of all people. We are praying that all people have food and the other things they need.

SHARING FAITH
with My Family

Sharing What I Learned

Look at the pictures below. Use each picture to tell your family what you learned in this chapter.

For All to See and Pray

Pray the Lord's Prayer with your family. Talk about what the words mean.

Our Father, who art in heaven,
hallowed be thy name;
thy kingdom come;
thy will be done on earth as it is in
  heaven.
Give us this day our daily bread;
and forgive us our trespasses
as we forgive those who trespass
  against us;
and lead us not into temptation,
but deliver us from evil.
Amen.

Visit Sadlier's
www.WeBelieveweb.com

Connect to the Catechism
For adult background and reflection, see paragraphs 543, 548, 2759, and 2776.

✝ We Gather in Prayer

Leader: Jesus, today we gather together to pray to you.

All: Jesus, we believe in you.

Leader: Jesus, you are wonderful.

All: Jesus, we praise you.

Leader: Jesus, you have done so much for us.

All: Jesus, we thank you.

Leader: Jesus, we want to follow you.

All: Jesus, help us to be your followers.

Jesus told his followers that he loved and cared for them.

WE GATHER

✝ *Jesus, help us to love and care for others.*

Look at the picture. What is happening?

WE BELIEVE

Jesus was a good teacher.
He wanted his followers to understand
what he was teaching.
He talked about things they knew about.

📖 John 10:2, 14

Read Along

One day Jesus was talking about shepherds.
He said, "I am the good shepherd, and I
know mine and mine know me." (John 10:14)

Jesus' followers knew all about
shepherds.
Shepherds stay with their sheep
night and day.
They take care of many sheep.
They know each of their sheep.
They do everything they can
to keep each one safe.

108

Jesus is our Good Shepherd.
He is with us night and day.
He knows each one of us.
He loves us very much.
He shows us ways to love
God and others.

Follow the path that shows ways to love God and others.

Be Kind.

Share.

Pray.

Be Fair.

What signs did you follow along the way?

WE RESPOND

How is Jesus like a shepherd to us?

Many people gathered to welcome and praise Jesus.

WE GATHER

✝ *Jesus, we praise you.*

Imagine special visitors are
coming to your school.
Act out how you will welcome them.

WE BELIEVE

Jesus visited many towns.
People welcomed him in different ways.
Some began to believe in Jesus.
They believed that Jesus was sent
by God.

📖 John 12:12–13

Read Along

Many people were in Jerusalem for a feast. They heard that Jesus was near the city, so they ran out to meet him. They waved palm branches in the air. They shouted, "Hosanna!
Blessed is he who comes in the name of the Lord." (John 12:13)

As Catholics...

During every Mass we pray Hosanna. We pray the same words the people did when they welcomed Jesus to Jerusalem. We show that we believe Jesus is the Son of God.

At Mass next week, praise Jesus for all he has done for us.

Hosanna is a word of praise.
The people that day were happy to see Jesus.
They shouted Hosanna to praise him.
They waved palm branches, too.

WE RESPOND

When do you praise Jesus?

🧍 Show some ways we can praise Jesus.

Jesus taught in the Temple in Jerusalem.

WE GATHER

✝ *Jesus, we want to listen to your teaching.*

Where do you live?
Talk about the cities or towns that are nearby.
Do you ever go to these places?
Why?

WE BELIEVE

Jerusalem is an important city to Jews.
They go there for special feasts.
They go there to pray.

Jerusalem was very important in Jesus' time, too.
Jesus went to Jerusalem.
He taught the people there.

The **Temple** was the holy place in Jerusalem where the Jewish people prayed.

 Luke 21:37–38

Read Along

During the week before Jesus died, he taught in the Temple area every day. "And all the people would get up early each morning to listen to him." (Luke 21:38)

Key Word

Temple the holy place in Jerusalem where the Jewish people prayed

WE RESPOND

Where do you go to pray and listen to Jesus' teaching?

🎵 **In the House of Our God**

In the House of our God,
   in the House of our God,
   we give praise to the Lord
   in the House of our God.

🤸 Make up actions
for the song.

Jesus died and rose.

WE GATHER

✝ *Jesus, thank you for your great love.*

Think about the people who love you very much.
How do they show their love for you?

WE BELIEVE

Jesus showed his love in many ways.
He cared for people.
He listened to them.
He shared God's love with them.

Jesus showed his love in a special way.
Jesus died so that all people could live in God's love.

📖 John 19:18, 25, 30, 42

Read Along

Jesus was nailed to a cross. Jesus' mother and a few followers were with him. Jesus died on the cross. After he died, some of his followers placed his body in a tomb.

On the third day after Jesus died, something wonderful happened.

 Matthew 28:1–7

Read Along

Early on Sunday morning, some women went to visit Jesus' tomb. They saw an angel sitting in front of the tomb. The angel said, "Do not be afraid!" (Matthew 28:5)

The angel told the women that Jesus had risen to new life. He told them to go tell the other followers.

Jesus died and rose to bring us new life. **Easter Sunday** is the special day we celebrate that Jesus Christ rose to new life. We pray Alleluia. Alleluia is another special word of praise.

WE RESPOND

How does your family celebrate Easter Sunday?

 Celebrate what Jesus did for us. Color the Alleluia garden.

Key Word

Easter Sunday the special day we celebrate that Jesus Christ rose to new life

Circle the correct answer.

1. The word people used to praise Jesus as he entered Jerusalem was _____.

Hosanna   Alleluia

2. The _____ was the place in Jerusalem where the Jewish people prayed.

Mountain   Temple

3. _____ died and rose to bring us new life.

Jesus   Peter

4. _____ is the special day we celebrate that Jesus Christ rose to new life.

Easter Sunday   Christmas Day

 Why did Jesus call himself the Good Shepherd?

 What are some things Jesus did to show his love for us? Draw or write your answer.

We Respond in Faith

 ## Reflect & Pray

Trace over the letters in the prayer.

Thank you,

Jesus, for rising to new life.

Key Words

Temple (p. 113)

Easter Sunday (p. 115)

Remember

- Jesus told his followers that he loved and cared for them.
- Many people gathered to welcome and praise Jesus.
- Jesus taught in the Temple in Jerusalem.
- Jesus died and rose.

OUR CATHOLIC LIFE

Respect for Workers

The Church teaches us to respect all workers. People work in our neighborhood to protect and care for us. Some of these workers are police officers, firefighters, people who help us to recycle, and those who help us to keep our neighborhoods clean.

We can ask Jesus, the Good Shepherd, to protect, help, and guide all workers.

SHARING FAITH
with My Family

Sharing What I Learned

Look at the pictures below. Use each picture to tell your family what you learned in this chapter.

Family Prayer Table

Set up a prayer table in your home. Place the table in a space where the family can easily gather or where people can pray by themselves. Look at the photo for ideas.

Invite the family to gather at the prayer table each night this week. Pray in your own words. Thank Jesus for all he has done for us.

Together, write your own family prayer here:

_____

_____

Visit Sadlier's

www.WeBelieveweb.com

Connect to the Catechism
For adult background and reflection, see paragraphs 754, 559, 584, and 638.

✝ We Gather in Prayer

Leader: Let us celebrate that Jesus Christ rose to new life.

♫ Sing for Joy

Sing and shout for joy, alleluia!
Sing and shout for joy, alleluia!
Sing and shout for joy, alleluia!
Alleluia! Alleluia!

Leader: Jesus wanted his followers to know that they would not be alone.

 Luke 24:36, 49

Read Along

Jesus did not want his followers to be afraid. He said to them, "Peace be with you." (Luke 24:36) Jesus promised his followers that he would send them a helper.

All: Jesus, thank you for sharing your peace and love.

The risen Jesus visited his followers.

WE GATHER

✝ *Alleluia, Jesus is risen!*

Think of a time when someone surprised you. How did they surprise you? What did you do?

WE BELIEVE

Jesus wanted his followers to know that he had risen. So he visited them. Here is a story about one of his visits.

 John 21:2–12

Read Along

One night Peter and some of Jesus' other followers went fishing. They were on the boat all night, but they did not catch any fish. Early the next morning, Jesus' followers saw someone on the shore. The person called out. He told them to put their nets into the water again.

Jesus' followers put the nets back into the water. They were surprised when they saw the nets filled with fish. They suddenly knew that the person on the shore was Jesus.

Peter was excited. He jumped into the water and swam to shore. The other followers came in the boat. Jesus said to them, "Come, have breakfast." (John 21:12)

👤 Number these sentences 1, 2, 3, 4 to retell the story.

_____ The followers knew the person was Jesus.
They went back to shore.

_____ Jesus asked his followers to have breakfast with him.

_____ Jesus' followers went fishing but did not catch any fish.

_____ Someone on shore called out and told them to put their nets in again.
They caught many fish.

WE RESPOND

👤 Imagine that your class is having breakfast with Jesus.
Act out what you would say and do.

121

Jesus Christ promised that the Holy Spirit would come to his followers.

WE GATHER

✝ *Jesus, help us to remember you always.*

Think about your family and friends. Why do you like to be with them?

Share ways you can remember them when they are not with you.

WE BELIEVE

The risen Christ was going to return to the Father in heaven. He did not want his followers to feel sad without him.

Jesus wanted his followers to remember him. He wanted them to tell others about God's love. He promised that the Holy Spirit would come to be with them.

The Holy Spirit would help Jesus' followers to:

- remember the things Jesus had said and done
- love others as Jesus had taught them
- tell others about Jesus.

After he made this promise, Jesus returned to his Father.

WE RESPOND

Ask the Holy Spirit to help you remember Jesus each day.

What is one thing you want to tell someone about Jesus?
Draw or write your answer here.
Who will you tell this to today?

The Holy Spirit was sent to Jesus' followers.

WE GATHER

✝ *Holy Spirit, be with us.*

Think of a time when you waited for someone to keep a promise. What did you do while you were waiting?

WE BELIEVE

After Jesus returned to heaven, his followers went to Jerusalem. They stayed together in a house there.
They prayed and waited for the Holy Spirit.

Here is what happened when the Holy Spirit came to Jesus' followers.

 Acts of the Apostles 2:1–4

Read Along

Early one morning, Jesus' followers were together in one place. Jesus' mother, Mary, was with them. Suddenly, they heard a sound like a strong wind. Then they saw what looked like flames of fire over each of them. "And they were all filled with the holy Spirit." (Acts of the Apostles 2:4)

Pentecost is the day the Holy Spirit came to Jesus' followers. We celebrate Pentecost fifty days after Easter Sunday. On this day we celebrate the coming of the Holy Spirit. Every day we remember that the Holy Spirit is with us.

 **Pentecost** the day the Holy Spirit came to Jesus' followers

WE RESPOND

How do you think Jesus' followers felt on Pentecost?

 Work with a partner. Make up a special tune or beat for this prayer.

You came on Pentecost.
You came to be with us.
Holy Spirit, we thank you
For coming to be with us.

As Catholics...

The Holy Spirit helps us to share God's love with others. God's love brings light and warmth to the world. This is why the Church often uses a picture of a flame or fire to remind us of the Holy Spirit. Fire gives us light and warmth.

Remember to pray to the Holy Spirit often.

The Holy Spirit is the third Person of the Blessed Trinity.

WE GATHER

✝ *God the Holy Spirit, we love you.*

Look at the pictures.
What prayer do you think the children are saying?

WE BELIEVE

The Sign of the Cross is a prayer to the Blessed Trinity.

God the Father is the first Person of the Blessed Trinity.
God the Son is the second Person of the Blessed Trinity.
God the Holy Spirit is the third Person of the Blessed Trinity.

It is important for us to remember that the Holy Spirit is God.
The Holy Spirit is always with us.

Here is a prayer we say to praise the Blessed Trinity.
In the prayer, *glory* is another word for praise.

Glory to the Father,
and to the Son,
and to the Holy Spirit:
as it was in the beginning,
is now, and will be for ever.
Amen.

WE RESPOND

 Together think of actions to use when you pray these words of praise.

Pray this prayer together now with actions.

Circle the correct answer.

1. Jesus visited his followers after he rose from the dead.

Yes   No   ?

2. Jesus promised that the Holy Spirit would come to his followers.

Yes   No   ?

3. The Holy Spirit came to Jesus' followers on Christmas.

Yes   No   ?

4. The Holy Spirit is the third Person of the Blessed Trinity.

Yes   No   ?

 Why did the risen Jesus visit his followers?

 What happened on Pentecost? Draw a picture. Write a sentence to tell about your picture.

We Respond in Faith

Reflect & Pray

Holy Spirit, you help me

Key Word

Pentecost (p. 125)

Remember

- The risen Jesus visited his followers.
- Jesus Christ promised that the Holy Spirit would come to his followers.
- The Holy Spirit was sent to Jesus' followers.
- The Holy Spirit is the third Person of the Blessed Trinity.

OUR CATHOLIC LIFE

Parish Get-Togethers

In this chapter you read about the time Jesus shared breakfast with his followers. Today, in many parishes, people join one another for breakfast after Sunday Mass. They talk with people they know. They also meet new people in the parish. They find out how different parish groups are helping others.

Sharing What I Learned

Look at the pictures below. Use each picture to tell your family what you learned in this chapter.

Sharing a Bible Story

Share the story about Jesus' visit with his followers on the beach. (See page 120.) Talk about what it must have been like to be with Jesus that morning.

Messages of God's Love

Make fish like the one on this page. Have each family member write a message on a fish about Jesus or the Holy Spirit. An example is *Jesus is with us always.*

Hide the fish in places where other family members will find them during the week. At the end of the week, gather to read all the messages.

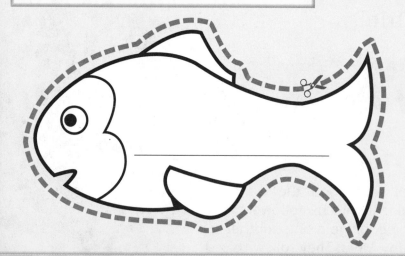

Visit Sadlier's

www.WeBelieveweb.com

Connect to the Catechism
For adult background and reflection, see paragraphs 641, 729, 730, and 732.

✝ We Gather in Prayer

Leader: Holy Spirit, we believe you are with us all the time. When we are excited or happy,

All: Holy Spirit, fill our  with love.

Leader: When we are sad or lonely,

All: Holy Spirit, fill our ♡ with love.

Leader: When we feel strong or brave,

All: Holy Spirit, fill our ♡ with love.

Leader: When we are tired or afraid,

All: Holy Spirit, fill our ♡ with love.

The Church began on Pentecost.

WE GATHER

✝ *Jesus, we believe in you.*

Think about something exciting that happened to you.
Who did you tell about it?

WE BELIEVE

On Pentecost Jesus' followers were excited.
The Holy Spirit had come to them.
They left the house where they were staying.
They wanted to tell people what had happened.

Acts of the Apostles 2:36–38, 41

Read Along

On Pentecost, Peter and the other apostles told people about Jesus. Peter told the people to believe in Jesus. He asked them to become Jesus' followers. If they did this, they would receive the Holy Spirit.

That day about three thousand people received the gift of the Holy Spirit. They became followers of Jesus.

This was the beginning of the Church.
The **Church** is all the people who believe in Jesus and follow his teachings.

Key Word

Church all the people who believe in Jesus and follow his teachings

WE RESPOND

Why is Pentecost a special day?

Add yourself to the picture. Pretend you are in the crowd. Tell what you are seeing and hearing.

133

The first members of the Church did many things together.

WE GATHER

✝ *Holy Spirit, make us one in Jesus.*

 Act out some things your family does together.

WE BELIEVE

The first members of the Church were like a close family.

They talked about Jesus' teachings. They learned together about ways to follow Jesus. They shared their money. They shared the things they had. They ate their meals together. They praised God together.

🎵 The First Church Members

("Here We Go 'Round the Mulberry Bush")

The first Church members shared
  their things,
shared their things, shared their things.
The first Church members shared
  their things
And we can do the same.

Sing this song again using these words:

The first Church members prayed
  together.

Together make up more
verses for this song.

WE RESPOND

How can you live like the first
Church members lived?

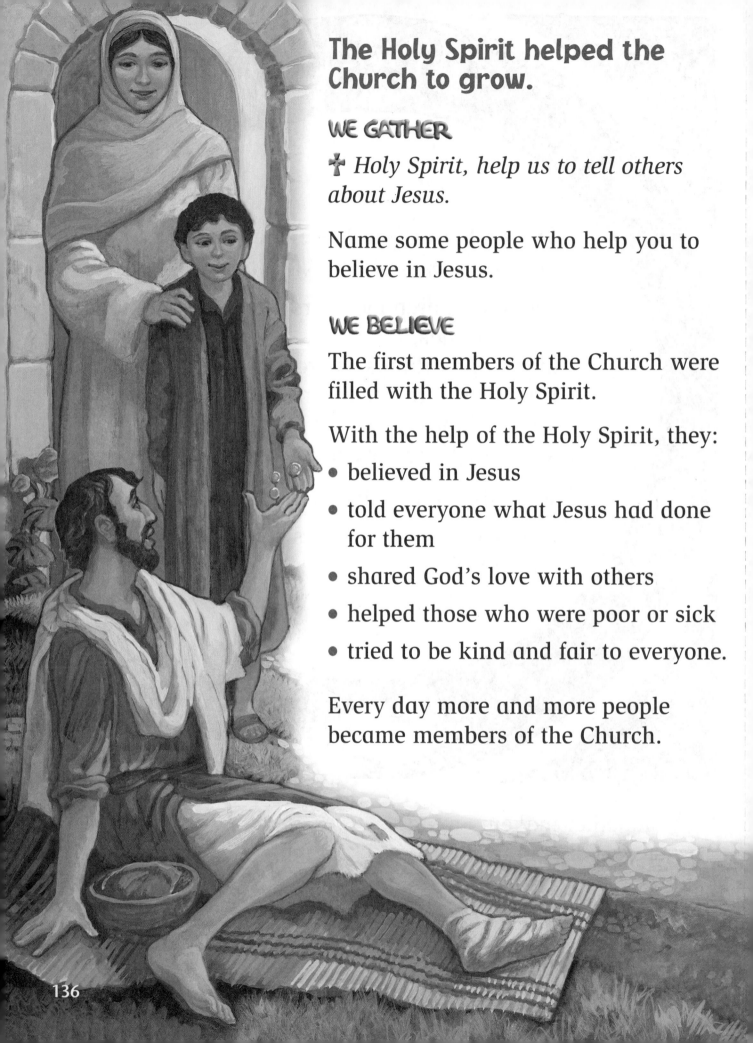

The Holy Spirit helped the Church to grow.

WE GATHER

✝ *Holy Spirit, help us to tell others about Jesus.*

Name some people who help you to believe in Jesus.

WE BELIEVE

The first members of the Church were filled with the Holy Spirit.

With the help of the Holy Spirit, they:

- believed in Jesus
- told everyone what Jesus had done for them
- shared God's love with others
- helped those who were poor or sick
- tried to be kind and fair to everyone.

Every day more and more people became members of the Church.

Q G A R M O S W

The Holy Spirit helps the Church to

_____ _____ _____ _____ .

Read the sentence above. What word is missing? Circle every other letter. Use the letters in the circles to write the missing word.

WE RESPOND

Together the first members of the Church prayed and asked the Holy Spirit to be with them.

Say a prayer to ask the Holy Spirit to be with you.

As Catholics...

After the Church began, Paul became a member, too. Like Peter, he told everyone he met about Jesus. Paul taught that all people were welcome in the Church.

On June 29, the Church honors Saint Peter and Saint Paul. On this day, we remember that Peter and Paul helped the Church to grow.

You can learn more about Saint Peter and Saint Paul in the Bible.

The Holy Spirit helps the Church today.

WE GATHER

✝ *God, may we grow in your love.*

🎵 Share the Light

Share the light of Jesus.
Share the light that shows the way.
Share the light of Jesus.
Share God's spirit today.
Share God's spirit today.

WE BELIEVE

The Holy Spirit is always with the Church.
We are members of the Church.
The Holy Spirit helps us to know that Jesus loves us.
The Holy Spirit helps us to live as Jesus taught us.

With the help of the Holy Spirit we:

- pray
- share with others
- care for those who are poor or sick
- show respect for all people
- learn more about Jesus and the Church
- follow the rules when working and playing with others.

WE RESPOND

What can you and your family do to live as Jesus taught us?

🎵 **Share the Light**

Share the love of Jesus.
Share the love that shows the way.
Share the love of Jesus.
Share God's spirit today.
Share God's spirit today.

Circle the correct answer.

1. On Pentecost many people became _____.

Jesus' followers   gifts of the
Holy Spirit

2. The first members of the Church _____.

were not friends   shared God's love

3. The _____ is all the people who believe
in Jesus and follow his teachings.

Holy Spirit   Church

4. The Holy Spirit _____ the Church to grow.

leaves   helps

 How did the first members of the
Church share God's love with others?

 Make a poster to show how the Holy
Spirit is with the Church today. Use
pictures from a magazine or draw your
own. Write words to go with the pictures.

We Respond in Faith

Reflect & Pray

Holy Spirit, guide us today.

Key Word

Church (p. 133)

Remember

- The Church began on Pentecost.
- The first members of the Church did many things together.
- The Holy Spirit helped the Church to grow.
- The Holy Spirit helps the Church today.

OUR CATHOLIC LIFE

Respecting All People

The Holy Spirit came to help all of Jesus' followers. We thank God for the many different people who are part of the Church. Here are some ways to say "thank you."

kam sa ham ni da (kahm-sah-hahm-nee-dah)   Korean
dziekuje (jehn-koo-yeh)   Polish
gracias (grah-see-ahs)   Spanish
ahsante (ah-sahn-tay)   Swahili
malo malo (mah-loh mah-loh)   Tongan

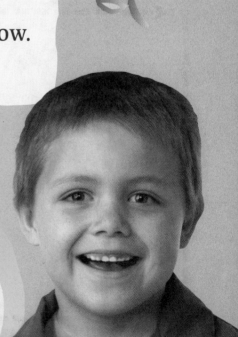

SHARING FAITH
with My Family

Sharing What I Learned

Look at the pictures below. Use each picture to tell your family what you learned in this chapter.

A Prayer Card

Cut out the prayer card. Ask each person in your family to write his or her initials on the flame. Pray to the Holy Spirit often.

Fold

All: Holy Spirit, we ask for your help.

Child: When we are excited or happy,

Child: When we are sad or lonely,

Child: When we are tired or afraid,

All: Holy Spirit, fill our hearts with love.

Visit Sadlier's

www.WeBelieveweb.com

 Connect to the Catechism
For adult background and reflection, see paragraphs 767, 2624, 768, and 798.

The Church Serves

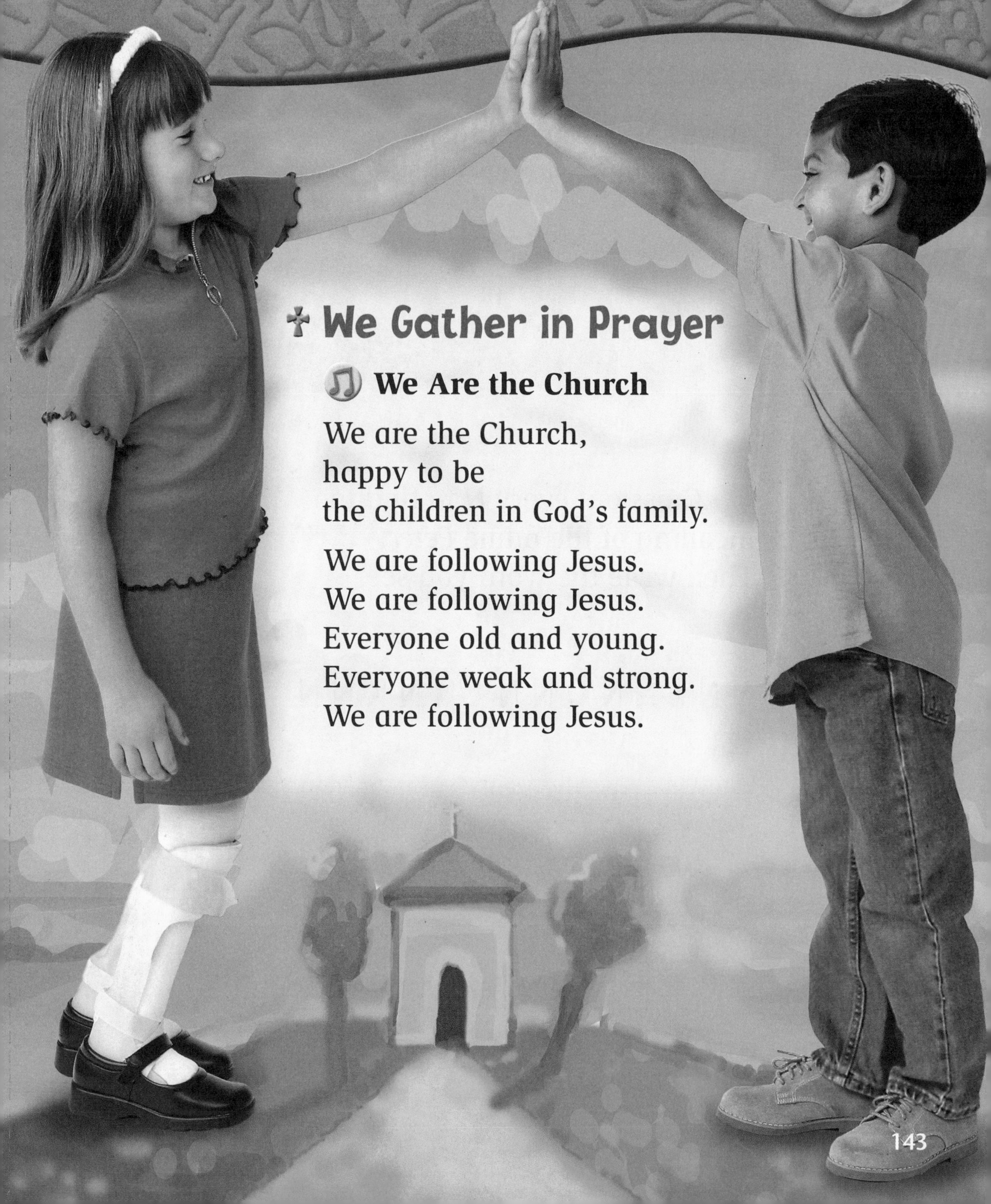

✝ **We Gather in Prayer**

🎵 **We Are the Church**

We are the Church,
happy to be
the children in God's family.

We are following Jesus.
We are following Jesus.
Everyone old and young.
Everyone weak and strong.
We are following Jesus.

The apostles led and cared for the Church.

WE GATHER

✝ *Thank you, God, for the Church.*

Some names have special meanings. Do you know any names with special meanings?

 Cross out every *N* to find the meaning of the name *Peter*. Then write the word you see.

N N R N N O N N C N N K N N

_____

WE BELIEVE

📖 Matthew 16:18

Read Along

One day Jesus asked Peter what he believed. Peter said he believed that Jesus was the Son of God. Jesus then said to Peter, "And so I say to you, you are Peter, and upon this rock I will build my church." (Matthew 16:18)

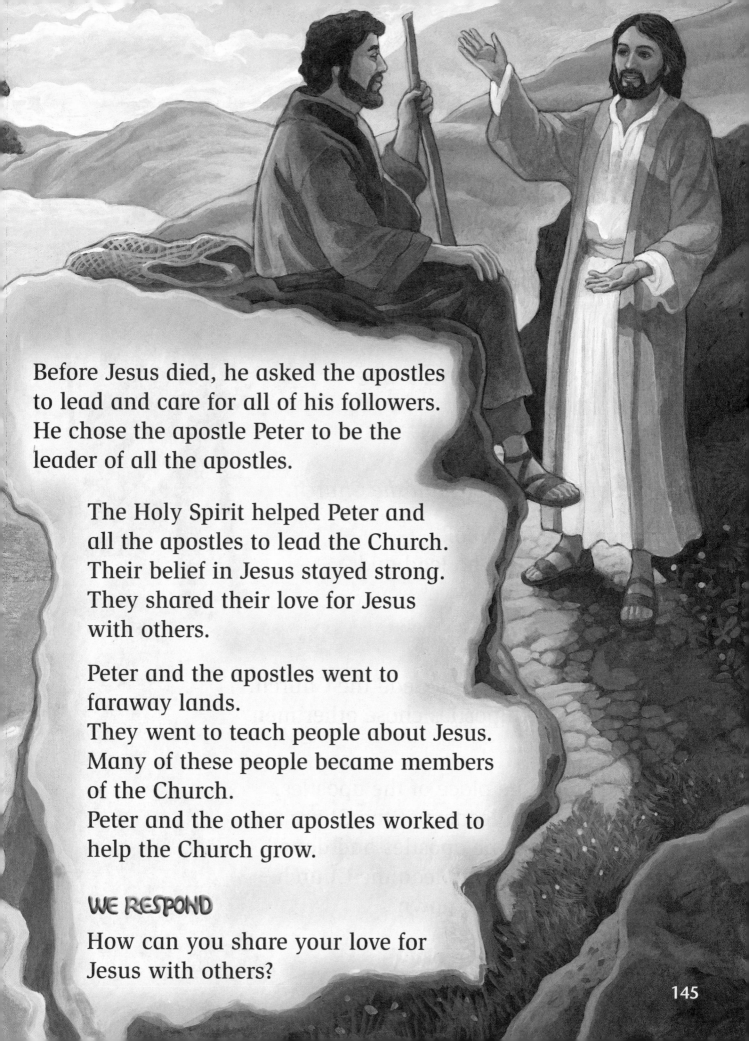

Before Jesus died, he asked the apostles
to lead and care for all of his followers.
He chose the apostle Peter to be the
leader of all the apostles.

The Holy Spirit helped Peter and
all the apostles to lead the Church.
Their belief in Jesus stayed strong.
They shared their love for Jesus
with others.

Peter and the apostles went to
faraway lands.
They went to teach people about Jesus.
Many of these people became members
of the Church.
Peter and the other apostles worked to
help the Church grow.

WE RESPOND

How can you share your love for
Jesus with others?

The bishops lead and care for the Church.

WE GATHER

✝ *Holy Spirit, please be with the Church.*

Think about your school.
Name some people who lead and
care for the students.

WE BELIEVE

Jesus chose the apostles to lead the Church.
In later years, the apostles chose other men
to lead the Church.

These men took the place of the apostles.
They were the new leaders of the Church.
They did the work the apostles had done.
They worked together to lead the Church.
These leaders became known
as bishops.

Bishops still lead and care for the Church today.
They teach about Jesus and the Church.
They pray with the people in their care.

Bishops take care of each diocese.
A diocese is made up of many members of the Church.
A bishop leads and cares for the people of his diocese.

Look at the pictures on this page.
Talk about ways the bishops are leading and caring for the members of the Church.

WE RESPOND

Who is your bishop?

Say a prayer and ask the Holy Spirit to help him.

The pope leads and cares for the whole Church.

WE GATHER

✝ *God the Father, bless the leaders of the Church.*

🧑 There are many people who are leaders. Match the leaders with the groups of people they work with.

a mayor • • a school

a principal • • a team

a coach • • a city

What are the ways these people work with others?

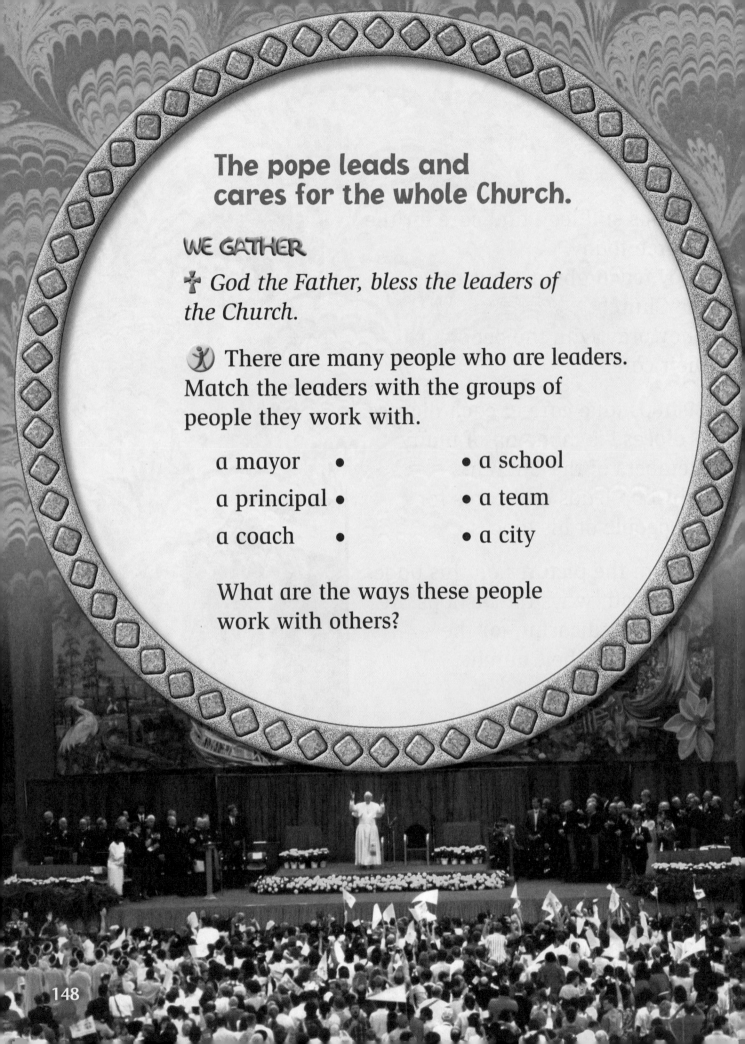

WE BELIEVE

The pope is the bishop of Rome in Italy.
He takes the place of Saint Peter.
Just like Saint Peter, he leads and
cares for the whole Church.

The pope works together with all
the bishops.

- He prays for and takes care of
  the Church.

- He teaches what Jesus taught.

- He visits people all over the world.

- He helps people everywhere.

- He cares for those in need.

The Holy Spirit helps the pope to
be a good leader.
The Holy Spirit helps the pope to
care for the Church.

WE RESPOND

Imagine that the pope will be
coming to visit your city or town.
You have the chance to meet him.
What do you think he might say
to you?

Pope John Paul II on Easter Sunday of 1991.

As Catholics...

The pope lives in the Vatican in
Rome, Italy. The main church
building of the Vatican is called
Saint Peter's. It is named for Peter,
the first leader of the Church.

People who are visiting from all
over the world gather outside
Saint Peter's every Wednesday.
There the pope speaks about Jesus
and the Church.

Find out the name of the pope.

The Church serves others.

WE GATHER

✝ *Jesus, help us love all the people of the world.*

🏃 Use the code to fill in the correct letters.

v	s	i	r	n	g	e
1	2	3	4	5	6	7

___ ___ ___ ___ ___ ___ ___
2 7 4 1 3 5 6

is another word for caring and helping.

WE BELIEVE

Jesus showed his followers ways to serve others.
He fed people who were hungry.
He spent time with people who needed him.
He took care of people who were sick.
He shared God's love with everyone.

Jesus said, "as I have done for you, you should also do." (John 13:15)

150

Members of the Church serve others.
Look at the pictures on these pages.
They show members of the Church.
How are they doing what
Jesus did?

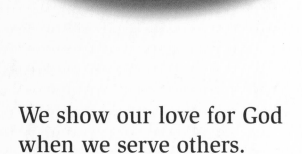

We show our love for God
when we serve others.

⚡ Which pictures show
how you and your family
can love and serve others?
Put a ♡ beside them.

WE RESPOND

What can you do in your
school to serve one another?

Circle Yes or No.
Circle ? if you do not know the answer.

1. Jesus chose Peter to be the leader of the apostles.

Yes   No   ?

2. We serve others by caring for and helping them.

Yes   No   ?

3. The pope is the leader of your town.

Yes   No   ?

4. The bishops do the work the apostles did.

Yes   No   ?

 TALK ABOUT IT

What are some ways the Church loves and serves others?

 ASSESSMENT

Draw or write the answer.
Members of the Church serve one another.
How does the pope serve? How do the bishops serve? How do we serve?

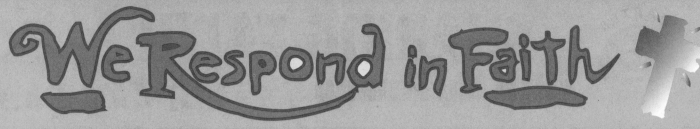

We Respond in Faith

Reflect & Pray

Talk to Jesus quietly. Tell him how you feel about serving others as he did. Draw a picture to show how you feel.

Remember

- The apostles led and cared for the Church.
- The bishops lead and care for the Church.
- The pope leads and cares for the whole Church.
- The Church serves others.

OUR CATHOLIC LIFE

A Catholic Missionary

Jesus told his followers to help people who were poor, hungry, or sick.

Mother Teresa began caring for people in India who were sick and homeless. She and her helpers fed the people and gave them a place to stay. Mother Teresa's helpers continue Jesus' work today. They are called the Missionaries of Charity. They lead us by showing the way to help others. They care for needy people in cities all over the world.

SHARING FAITH
with My Family

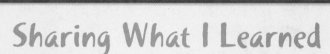

Sharing What I Learned

Look at the pictures below. Use each picture to tell your family what you learned in this chapter.

Talking Together

Talk together about the way your family would feel if you could meet the pope. Write a question that your family would like to ask the pope.

_____

_____

_____

_____

A Prayer for the Church

Pray this prayer together.

Holy Spirit, watch over (name), our pope.
Protect and bless (name), our bishop.
Holy Spirit, bless all people,
old and young, rich and poor,
those who live nearby and
those who live far away,
the sick and the healthy.
We ask you to hear our prayer.

Connect to the Catechism
For adult background and reflection,
see paragraphs 858, 862, 881, and 1942.

Advent

Come, Lord Jesus!
Be with us.

WE GATHER

Think about a time your family was waiting to celebrate a special day.

What did you do?

How did you feel?

WE BELIEVE

The Church has a special time of waiting. Each year we wait for the coming of the Son of God. This waiting time is called Advent.

The word *Advent* means "coming." Each year during Advent we prepare. We get ready for the coming of God's Son, Jesus. We get ready to celebrate his birth at Christmas.

There are four weeks in Advent. The Church celebrates these four weeks in different ways. One way is by lighting candles on an Advent wreath.

On the Advent wreath there is one candle for each week. The light from the candles reminds us that Jesus is the Light of the World.

We pray as we light the candles on the Advent wreath. We remember that Jesus is with us. We prepare to celebrate his birth at Christmas.

 Color the flames on each candle on the Advent wreath.

Ask Jesus to shine his light on all the world. Sing together.

🎵 **Advent Song**

Candle, candle burning bright,
shining in the cold winter night.
Candle, candle burning bright,
fill our hearts with Christmas light.

WE RESPOND

During Advent we can share Jesus' light with others. With your classmates talk about ways you can do this.

Write about or draw a picture of one way.

✝ We Respond in Prayer

Leader: Let us praise God and listen to his word.

Reader: Jesus said, "I am the light of the world. Whoever follows me will not walk in darkness, but will have the light of life." (John 8:12)

The Gospel of the Lord.

All: Praise to you, Lord Jesus Christ.

Leader: Jesus, help us to make the world bright with your life.

All: Come, Lord Jesus!

🎵 **Jesus, Come to Us**

Jesus, come to us,
lead us to your light.
Jesus, be with us,
for we need you.

SHARING FAITH
with My Family

Sharing What I Learned

Look at the pictures below. Use each picture to tell your family what you learned in this chapter.

Advent Prayer Partners

Ask each member of your family to write his or her name on a slip of paper. Then have each person choose a name. That person is your Advent "prayer partner." Pray especially for your prayer partner. Make that person a special card for Christmas.

Family Prayer

Keep a candle on the table when you share family meals. Before each meal, ask a grown-up to light the candle. Then pray together, "Come, Lord Jesus."

Visit Sadlier's

www.WEBELIEVEweb.com

Connect to the Catechism
For adult background and reflection, see paragraph 524.

"For a child is born to us, a son is given us."

Isaiah 9:5

At Christmas the Church celebrates the birth of Jesus.

WE GATHER

What do you think of when you think of Christmas?

WE BELIEVE

Christmas is a special time. During Christmas, we celebrate the birth of the Son of God. We celebrate God's greatest gift to us, his Son, Jesus.

 Act out this Christmas play.

Narrator: Before Jesus was born, the ruler wanted to count all the people. Each man had to go back to the town his family came from to be counted. Joseph's family was from Bethlehem. So Joseph and Mary made the long journey to Bethlehem.

Joseph: Here we are, Mary! We're finally in Bethlehem! You must be very tired.

Mary: I'm all right, Joseph. It was a long journey. It will be so good to rest!

Joseph: Here is an inn. Maybe we can stay here.

Innkeeper: Not another traveler! What do you want?

Joseph: We need a place to stay.

Innkeeper: Sorry, there's no room left.

Joseph: Please, sir. My wife needs a place to rest. We're going to have a baby soon.

Innkeeper's Wife: We do have a place where the animals are kept. I put down fresh straw this morning. At least you can try to keep warm there.

Mary: Thank you for your kindness. May God bless you!

Narrator: So Joseph and Mary stayed there. Joseph made a place for the baby in the animals' feedbox. It is called a manger. He filled the manger with clean straw.

That night, Jesus was born. Mary and Joseph were filled with joy. They wrapped the baby in swaddling clothes and laid him in the manger.

Read Along

During Christmas, we sing with joy. Jesus has brought light and love into the world. He is with us now and forever.

Christmas is a time to honor the Holy Family. We remember the love of Mary and Joseph. We remember their love and care for Jesus.

WE RESPOND

Christmas is a time to share God's love with family and friends. Each thing you do for others can be a gift.

 Color each gift box that shows a way you can share God's love. Then add your own way.

Each day during this time of year try to do these things.

Help keep my home clean.

Get along with everyone.

Pray for my family.

Share my things.

✝ We Respond in Prayer

Leader: Let us give thanks for the Son of God brings light and love into the world. Rejoice in the Lord always.

All: Rejoice in the Lord always.

Reader: Let us listen to a reading from the Bible.

"The people who walked in darkness
     have seen a great light;
Upon those who dwelt in the land
     of gloom
     a light has shone.
You have brought them abundant joy
     and great rejoicing." (Isaiah 9:1–2)

The word of the Lord.

All: Thanks be to God.

🎵 Joy to the World

Joy to the world!
The Lord is come;
Let earth receive her King;
Let ev'ry heart prepare him room,
And heav'n and nature sing,
And heav'n and nature sing,
And heav'n, and heav'n and nature sing.

SHARING FAITH
with My Family

Sharing What I Learned

Look at the pictures below. Use each picture to tell your family what you learned in this chapter.

For All to See and Pray

Color the holly leaves on the wreath green. Color the berries red. Then pray this blessing with your family.

God our Father, bless our wreath. The green leaves remind us that your love never ends. Its red berries remind us that Jesus died and rose for us. Thank you for sending Jesus, your Son, to be with us always. Amen.

 Connect to the Catechism
For adult background and reflection, see paragraph 463.

Fill in the circle beside the correct answer.

1. The Church is all the people who believe in Jesus and follow his teachings.

○ Yes   ○ No

2. Jesus chose John to be the leader of the apostles.

○ Yes   ○ No

3. Jesus' followers believed he was the Son of God.

○ Yes   ○ No

4. Jesus taught his followers how to _____.

○ pray   ○ read

5. Jesus told us that he was the _____.

○ pope   ○ Good Shepherd

6. The Holy Spirit is the _____ Person of the Blessed Trinity.

○ first   ○ third

Tell why the Lord's Prayer is a special prayer.

Match each sentence to the correct picture.

- Jesus invited people to be his followers.

- Jesus taught his followers to pray.

- The first members of the Church shared God's love with others.

- The Holy Spirit came to Jesus' followers on Pentecost.

We Belong to the Church

SHARING FAITH as a Family

What Every Parent Should Know About the Media

American children watch an estimated 3–5 hours of television a day. Such a statistic is reason for parents to be media-savvy and to become pro-active about the use of media in the home. Here are some areas for consideration.

Media requires an audience. The choice of being an active or passive consumer is up to us. "Talking back" is a way of critically evaluating what we are watching. Ask yourself, "Does the message support or undermine the values that we as a family hold dear?"

Media creates its own reality. With rare exception, everything on television or in the movies is edited, usually to create a specific effect. Because young children are so literal, they take what they see at face value. Thus, what adults can dismiss as fantasy, children take to heart.

Monitor what they watch by restricting choices and using credible review and ratings systems.

Media is a business. Every form of media, from TV to the Internet, has something to sell. Children are easy targets for such marketing. Talk to your child about such sales techniques and, together, develop a response to it.

Active participation in the media doesn't mean we can't enjoy it. It does mean we take responsibility for what we consume and we help our children to do the same.

At www.webelieveweb.com you'll find ways you can use media to interact in positive ways with your child.

From the Catechism

[The Christian family] "is a community of faith, hope and charity; it assumes singular importance in the Church."

(Catechism of the Catholic Church, 2204)

From the Bible

"Beloved, let us love one another, because love is of God; everyone who loves is begotten by God and knows God."

(1 John 4:7)

Be a "Light of the World" Family

Jesus, the Light of the World, calls us to share his light by sharing his peace and forgiveness with others. Your family shows peace and forgiveness to one another in many ways—saying, "I'm sorry," helping with the dishes, taking phone messages, sharing the remote control, etc.

Use the space below to record some ways your family shows how you share Jesus' light in your home.

What Your Child Will Learn in Unit 3

In Unit 3, the children will learn to be more appreciative that they are members who belong to the Church. The parish is presented as a family of believers who help each other and all people. One way members can be strengthened in their faith in God is through the sacraments. The children will learn the meaning of a sacrament and will be able to name the seven sacraments. The sacrament of Baptism is highlighted for the first graders. As followers of Jesus, the children will grow in their understanding of Jesus' message of peace and forgiveness.

Plan & Preview

▶ You might have a note card handy for a thank you card. *(Chapter 15 Family Page)*

▶ Obtain a piece of cardboard or stiff paper. *(Chapter 16 Family Page)*

▶ Fill a glass bowl or clear container with water. *(Chapter 17 Family Page)*

We Belong to a Parish

✝ We Gather in Prayer

Leader: Jesus' followers said to him, "Lord, teach us to pray." (Luke 11:1) Let us join together and pray the prayer Jesus taught.

All: Our Father, who art in heaven, hallowed be thy name; thy kingdom come; thy will be done on earth as it is in heaven. Give us this day our daily bread; and forgive us our trespasses as we forgive those who trespass against us; and lead us not into temptation but deliver us from evil. Amen.

Our parish is like a family.

WE GATHER

✝ *God, thank you for the Church.*

 Act out some ways families spend time together.

WE BELIEVE

We belong to the Catholic Church. We are Catholics. We belong to a parish.

A **parish** is a group of Catholics who join together to share God's love. They pray, celebrate, and work together. The people who belong to a parish are like a family.

We do many things with our parish.

- We praise and thank God.
- We share God's love with others.
- We learn how to be followers of Jesus.
- We work together to help people.

Key Word

parish a group of Catholics who join together to share God's love

WE RESPOND

What things do you like to do with your parish?

 Finish the card.
Write your name and the name of your parish.

_____

I, _____,

belong to

_____

_____ Parish.

We gather together to worship.

WE GATHER

✝ *O God, we give you thanks and praise.*

Find out where these people are going. Connect the dots.

WE BELIEVE

Our parish joins together to celebrate God's love. We **worship** God. We give him thanks and praise.

Every week we gather to worship God in our parish church. Our parish church is a holy place. God is with us there in a special way.

Key Word

worship to give God
thanks and praise

Look at the picture.
Talk about what you see.

WE RESPOND

How does your parish worship God?

🎵 Open Our Hearts

God, we come to worship you:

Chorus
Open our hearts to listen to you.
Open our hearts to listen to you.

God, your love is always true:

(Chorus)

We work together as a parish.

✝ *Jesus, please help the members of our parish.*

Who are some of the people you know in your parish?

WE BELIEVE

The leader of a parish is called the **pastor**. The pastor is a priest.

The pastor leads us in worship. He teaches us about Jesus. He helps us to care for one another.

Who is the pastor of your parish? Write his name here.

_____

- -

_____

_____

- -

_____

Other leaders in the parish work with the pastor. Together they help the parish family.

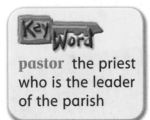

Key Word

pastor the priest who is the leader of the parish

Many people work together in our parish. Some help us to worship God. Some teach us about God. Some work with us to care for those who are sick or in need.

WE RESPOND

Talk about ways you thank the pastor of your parish.

Other people work in and help lead your parish. How can you thank them?

As Catholics...

Catechists teach the Catholic faith to the children, youth, and adults of the parish. They are very important people in the parish. They teach about Jesus and the Church. They help us to be friends and followers of Jesus.

Who teaches you about the Catholic faith?

Our parish helps many people.

WE GATHER

✝ *Jesus, help our parish to do your work.*

How would you help? Act out what you can do.

- Your friend forgot his lunch.
- Your sister spilled milk on the table.
- Your friend fell and got hurt.

WE BELIEVE

In our parish we help one another. We try to spend time with our parish family. We may join them for picnics or dinners. We help people of our parish who are in need.

Our parish helps other people, too. We gather food and clothes for those who are poor. We send money to those who are in need.

Our parish cares for those who are sick. People from the parish visit them. We can pray for them. We can also send them cards.

WE RESPOND

 Circle one way you will help your parish this week.

- Join in singing and praying.
- Keep the parish buildings neat and clean.
- Pray for my parish.
- Be kind and friendly.

Together say a prayer for all those who are in need.

Circle the correct answer.
Circle ? if you do not know the answer.

1. A parish prays, celebrates, and works together.

   Yes   No   ?

2. A parish church is a holy place.

   Yes   No   ?

3. The priest who leads a parish is called the president.

   Yes   No   ?

4. The people in a parish help other people.

   Yes   No   ?

 **TALK ABOUT IT** What do the people in your parish do together?

 **ASSESSMENT** Make a poster to welcome others to your parish. Show some of the ways your parish is like a family.

We Respond in Faith

Reflect & Pray

Jesus, I want to help my parish family this week. I want to

Key Words

parish (p. 173)
worship (p. 175)
pastor (p. 176)

Remember

- Our parish is like a family.
- We gather together to worship.
- We work together as a parish.
- Our parish helps many people.

OUR CATHOLIC LIFE

Feeding the Hungry

People who do not have homes or jobs need food. Many parish families join together to help these people in need.

Some parish families work in soup kitchens. They cook and serve meals to people who come to their parish hungry. Some parish families collect food. They fill boxes and bags with canned food. Then they take the food to those in need.

SHARING FAITH
with My Family

Sharing What I Learned

Look at the pictures below. Use each picture to tell your family what you learned in this chapter.

Parish Helpers

Talk about the people who help your parish family. Talk about what they do to help. Together make a thank-you card or sign to send to one of these helpers. Use this space to plan what you will write.

_____

_____

We Belong

Pray this prayer every day this week.

God, thank you for our parish family.
Help us to join together to share your love.

Visit Sadlier's

www.WeBelieveweb.com

Connect to the Catechism
For adult background and reflection, see paragraphs 2179, 2182, and 2444.

We Celebrate the Sacraments

✝ We Gather in Prayer

Leader: There are many signs of God's love for us. We see God's love in his gifts of creation and in one another. Jesus is the greatest sign of God's love. He shares God's life and love with us. Let us celebrate God's love for us.

🎵 We Celebrate With Joy

Chorus

We celebrate with joy and gladness
We celebrate God's love for us.
We celebrate with joy and gladness
God with us today. (Clap 2 times.)
God with us today. (Clap 2 times.)

God before us. God behind us.
God in everything we do.
God before us. God behind us.
God in all we do. (Chorus)

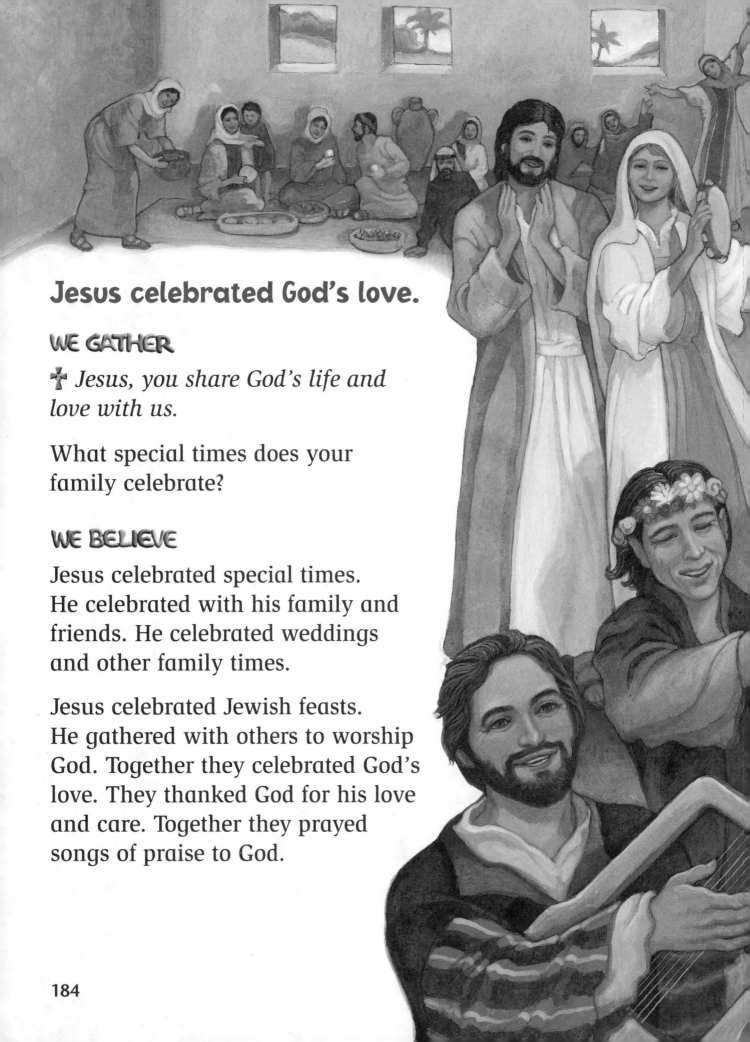

Jesus celebrated God's love.

WE GATHER

✝ *Jesus, you share God's life and love with us.*

What special times does your family celebrate?

WE BELIEVE

Jesus celebrated special times. He celebrated with his family and friends. He celebrated weddings and other family times.

Jesus celebrated Jewish feasts. He gathered with others to worship God. Together they celebrated God's love. They thanked God for his love and care. Together they prayed songs of praise to God.

Here is one of these songs of praise to God.

"Shout joyfully to the LORD, all you lands;
  worship the LORD with cries of gladness;
  come before him with joyful song."
Psalm 100:1–2

We can pray these words of praise.
Sometimes we pray them when we
worship God as a parish.

WE RESPOND

Pray together the song of praise
above. Make up actions for the prayer.

How else will you celebrate
God's love today?

We celebrate God's love.

WE GATHER

✝ *God, we praise you for your love.*

🧑 Pretend that someone your family loves is coming to your home. How will you celebrate this visit? Act out what you will say and do.

WE BELIEVE

We gather with our parish family to celebrate God's love. We gather to worship together.

When we worship, we thank God for sending his Son. We remember the things that Jesus said and did. We ask the Holy Spirit to help us.

When we worship, we use special words and actions.

🧑 Color in the letters of these special words we pray.

Alleluia
Amen

When we worship God together,
we do different things.
We ask God to be with us.
We pray using words, songs,
and actions.
We listen to God's word.

WE RESPOND

What are some ways you
pray and thank God?

Stand and pray.

Alleluia. God, we praise you.
God, we thank you.
God, we love you. Amen.

 Draw yourself worshiping God
with your parish.

Jesus gave us the sacraments.

WE GATHER

✝ *Jesus, thank you for giving us signs of God's love.*

Think about the people you love. How can you show them your love?

WE BELIEVE

God loves us very much. He loves us so much he sent his Son to us. Jesus, the Son of God, shares God's life and love with us.

Jesus wants each of us to share in God's life. So he gave us seven special signs of God's life and love. The seven special signs Jesus gave us are called sacraments. A **sacrament** is a special sign given to us by Jesus.

We gather with our parish family to celebrate the sacraments. Jesus is with us each time we celebrate.

WE RESPOND

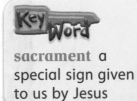 Trace over the words in this prayer.

Jesus, thank you for the

_____

seven sacraments.

Thank you for the

_____

signs of God's life and love.

Key Word

sacrament a
special sign given
to us by Jesus

The Church celebrates seven sacraments.

✝ *Jesus, you are with us always.*

🎵 **Celebrate God**

Celebrate God with your hands.
Celebrate God with your voice.
Celebrate God in all that you do.
And God will be with you.

WE BELIEVE

The Church celebrates seven sacraments.
We receive the sacraments at different
times in our lives. But Jesus shares
God's life with us in each of the sacraments.
Each sacrament helps us to grow closer to God.

Look at the pictures. Each one shows
a sacrament that is being celebrated.

Baptism

Confirmation

Eucharist

Penance and Reconciliation

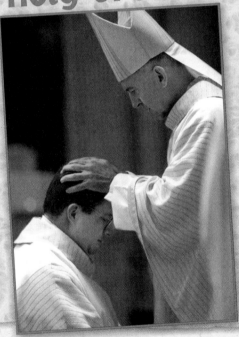

Anointing of the Sick

Matrimony

Holy Orders

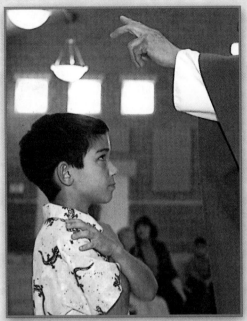

WE RESPOND

Talk about what is happening in each picture on these pages. Do these pictures remind you of things you have seen in your parish?

As Catholics...

We use the gifts of God's creation during the celebration of the sacraments. For example, water and oils are used to bless us. Light from candles reminds us that Jesus is with us. Bread made from wheat and wine made from grapes are used, too.

With your family, thank God for all he has given us.

Review

Circle the correct answer.

1. Jesus shares God's life with us in _____ of the sacraments.

each   some

2. _____ gave us the sacraments.

Peter   Jesus

3. The Church celebrates _____ sacraments.

seven   ten

4. _____ is a special word we use when we worship God.

Hello   Alleluia

TALK ABOUT IT What are some of the special words and actions we use to worship God?

ASSESSMENT Make a banner that shows how we celebrate God's love.

We Respond in Faith

Reflect & Pray

God, I will celebrate your love this week by

Key Word

sacrament (p. 189)

Remember

- Jesus celebrated God's love.
- We celebrate God's love.
- Jesus gave us the sacraments.
- The Church celebrates seven sacraments.

OUR CATHOLIC LIFE

Songs of Praise and Love

God has given some people a talent for music. Some people use their gift to write songs of praise and thanks to God. We sing some of these songs when our parish family gathers to worship God. We sing these songs when we celebrate the sacraments.

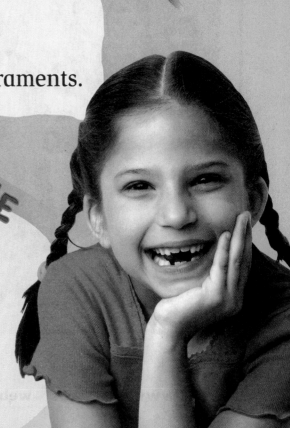

SHARING FAITH
with My Family

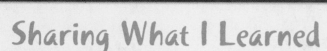

Sharing What I Learned

Look at the pictures below. Use each picture to tell your family what you learned in this chapter.

Jesus Is with Us

Get your family together. Cut out this picture of Jesus. Glue it to a piece of cardboard or stiff paper. Stand this picture on your prayer table. Talk with your family about Jesus and the sacraments he gave us. Remember they are ways to celebrate God's love.

Pray Together

Jesus, thank you for the special times we share together.

Visit Sadlier's

www.WEBELIEVEweb.com

Connect to the Catechism
For adult background and reflection, see paragraphs 583, 1083, 1084, and 1113.

✝ We Gather in Prayer

Leader: God the Father,
All: We praise you.

Leader: Jesus, Son of God,
All: Show us how to live.

Leader: God the Holy Spirit,
All: Help us each day.

The Church welcomes new members at Baptism.

WE GATHER

✝ *God, we are your children.*

Look at the picture of the Stanik family. What do you think Father Marcos is saying to them?

WE BELIEVE

Father Marcos and the whole parish are welcoming the Stanik family. They are bringing their baby to celebrate the sacrament of Baptism. The baby's name is Leo.

In Baptism, Leo will become a child of God. He will become a member of the Church.

Baptism is the sacrament in which we become children of God and members of the Church. Baptism is the first sacrament we receive.

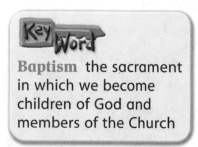

Key Word

Baptism the sacrament in which we become children of God and members of the Church

When we were baptized, we became children of God. We became members of the Church, too. We celebrated Baptism with our parish family. They welcomed us into the Catholic Church.

As Catholics...

We receive the sacrament of Baptism once. Some people are baptized when they are babies. Others are baptized when they are older. Older children, teenagers, or adults are usually baptized at a celebration on the night before Easter Sunday.

How old were you when you were baptized?

WE RESPOND

Why do you think Baptism is so important?

🎵 We Are the Church

We are the Church,
happy to be
the children in God's family.
(Repeat)

At Baptism we receive God's life.

WE GATHER

✞ *God, we want to grow in your love.*

Look at the picture. What does the plant need so it can grow? Add to the picture what the plant needs.

Why is water important?

WE BELIEVE

Water is an important sign of Baptism. During the sacrament we are placed in water, or water is poured on us.

This happens in a special place in our parish church. This place is called the baptismal pool or font.

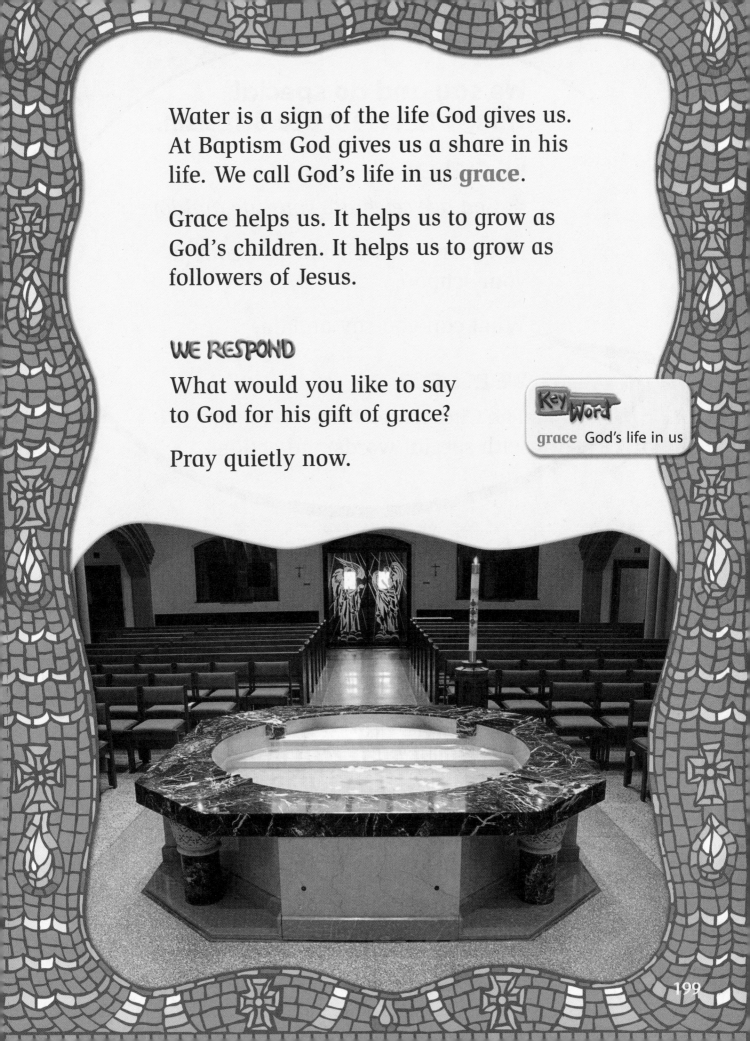

Water is a sign of the life God gives us. At Baptism God gives us a share in his life. We call God's life in us **grace**.

Grace helps us. It helps us to grow as God's children. It helps us to grow as followers of Jesus.

WE RESPOND

What would you like to say to God for his gift of grace?

Pray quietly now.

Key Word

grace God's life in us

We say and do special things to celebrate Baptism.

WE GATHER

✝ *God, we celebrate your life and love.*

How can you welcome someone to your school?

What can you say and do?

WE BELIEVE

The Church celebrates Baptism with special words and actions.

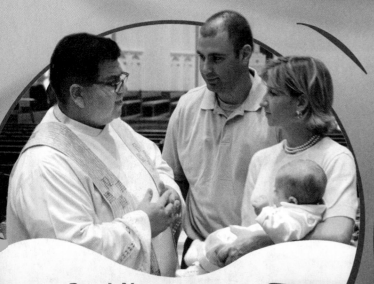

Read Along

Leo's Baptism

Father Marcos talked to Leo's family about the celebration.

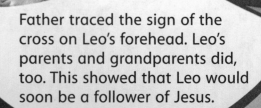

Father traced the sign of the cross on Leo's forehead. Leo's parents and grandparents did, too. This showed that Leo would soon be a follower of Jesus.

Father placed Leo in the water of the baptismal pool three times. He said the words of Baptism:

Leo, I baptize you in the name
 of the Father,
and of the Son,
and of the Holy Spirit.

Each of us was baptized with water and these words, too.

WE RESPOND

What would you like to ask your family about the celebration of your Baptism?

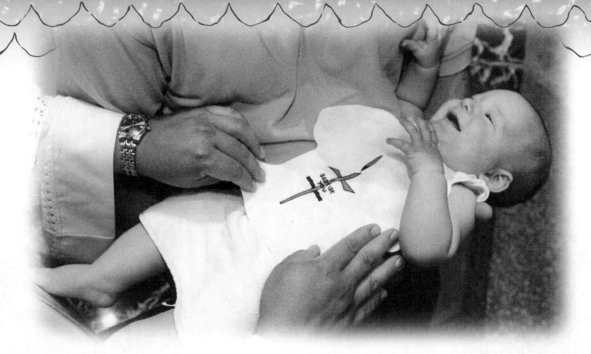

In Baptism we are joined to Jesus and one another.

WE GATHER

✝ *In the name of the Father, and of the Son, and of the Holy Spirit. Amen.*

Talk about what happened at the beginning of Leo's Baptism.

WE BELIEVE

These words and actions were also a part of Leo's Baptism.

Read Along

A white garment was put on Leo. Father prayed that Leo would always live as a follower of Jesus.

A candle was given to Leo's family. Someone from the family lit the candle. Father prayed that Leo would always walk in the light of Christ.

Everyone prayed the Lord's Prayer.

These same words and actions were part of the celebration of our Baptism.

As baptized members of the Church, we help one another to follow Jesus. We share in God's life together. We share our beliefs.

WE RESPOND

What will you do to live as a follower of Jesus?

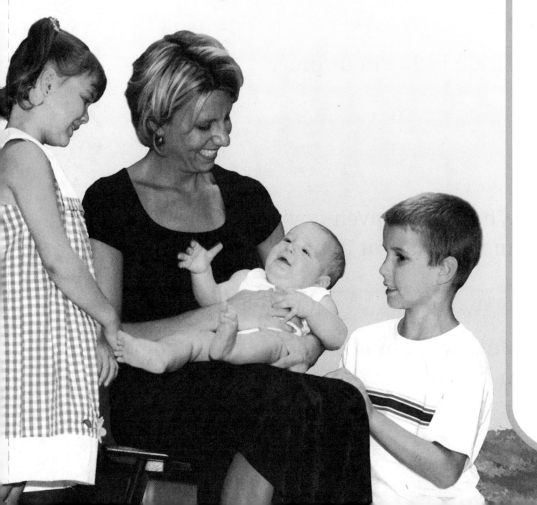 Decorate this candle.

I will walk in the light of Christ.

203

Circle the correct answer.
Circle ? if you do not know the answer.

1. Baptism is the third sacrament we receive.

Yes　　　　No　　　　?

2. Water is an important sign of Baptism.

Yes　　　　No　　　　?

3. In Baptism we become members of the Church.

Yes　　　　No　　　　?

4. We call God's life in us grace.

Yes　　　　No　　　　?

 **Why are we given a white garment and a candle at Baptism?**

 Make a card for someone who is going to be baptized. Tell why Baptism is a happy celebration.

We Respond in Faith

 Reflect & Pray

Pray quietly. Thank God for the gift of his life, grace.

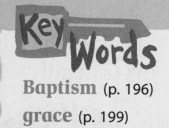 **Key Words**

Baptism (p. 196)

grace (p. 199)

Remember

- The Church welcomes new members at Baptism.
- At Baptism we receive God's life.
- We say and do special things to celebrate Baptism.
- In Baptism we are joined to Jesus and one another.

OUR CATHOLIC LIFE

Holy Water

Holy Water is water that has been blessed by a priest. When the priest blesses the water, he traces a cross over the water with his hand. He says a special prayer. The priest blesses the water in the baptismal pool or font during the sacrament of Baptism. Holy water is also kept in a special container in church.

Sometimes when our parish is worshiping God, the priest sprinkles us with holy water. He does this to remind us of our Baptism. We make the sign of the cross at this time.

SHARING FAITH
with My Family

Sharing What I Learned

Look at the pictures below. Use each picture to tell your family what you learned in this chapter.

Remembering Baptism

Help your family remember what happens at Baptism.

Pour water into a glass bowl or clear container. Put the bowl on the table that you use for family meals. Remember together that water is an important sign of Baptism.

Before meals this week, ask family members to dip their fingers into the water. Then pray the Sign of the Cross.

Talk about your family's Baptism celebrations. Look at pictures and videos of these celebrations.

Visit Sadlier's

www.WeBelieveweb.com

Connect to the Catechism
For adult background and reflection, see paragraphs 1267, 1265, 1234, and 1271.

We Are Followers of Jesus

18

✝ We Gather in Prayer

Leader: Let us listen to the word of God.

 John 8:12

Read Along

One day Jesus was talking to a crowd. He said to them, "I am the light of the world. Whoever follows me will not walk in darkness but will have the light of life."

🎵 Walk in the Light

Jesus is the Light for all:
Walk, walk in the light!
We follow him as we hear
  his call.
Walk, walk in the light!

Walk, walk in the light!
(Sing 3 times.)

Walk in the light
  of the Lord!

Jesus is the Light of the World.

WE GATHER

✝ *Jesus, we want to follow you.*

Think about things that give light.
How does the light of the sun help us?
How does a flashlight help us?
How do the lights in our homes help us?

WE BELIEVE

 John 8:12

Read Along

One day Jesus was talking to a crowd. He said to them,
"I am the light of the world. Whoever follows me will not
walk in darkness but will have the light of life." (John 8:12)

We believe that Jesus is the Light of the
World. He helps us to see what God's
love is like. He shares God's life with us.

Jesus wants us to follow him. If we
follow him, we will have life with God.

WE RESPOND

What are some ways you can follow Jesus?

 Draw a picture to show that Jesus is the Light of the World.

We receive the light of Christ.

WE GATHER

✝ *Jesus, help us to share your light.*

Think about someone who was kind to you.
What did the person do or say?
How did this make you feel?

WE BELIEVE

When we are baptized, we receive the light of Christ. We are told to "walk always as children of the light."

As children of the light, we are followers of Jesus. We:

• believe in Jesus

• act as Jesus wants us to

• love one another.

We show others the light of Christ when we:

- help our family and friends
- share what we have with others
- care about the way others feel.

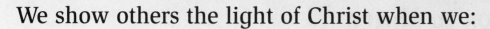

WE RESPOND

How can you show others that you have received the light of Christ?

🎵 **Walk in the Light**

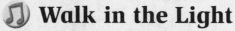

We walk together in Jesus' light:
Walk, walk in the light!
And let our own light shine so bright.
Walk, walk in the light!

Walk, walk in the light! (Sing 3 times.)
Walk in the light of the Lord!

Jesus asks us to share his peace.

WE GATHER

✝ *Jesus, we want to share your peace.*

Have you ever heard someone talk about peace? When?

WE BELIEVE

Jesus wanted his followers to be at peace. He wanted them to live in God's love. He wanted them to get along with one another. He wanted them to show love for one another.

 Matthew 5:1, 9

Read Along

One day Jesus went up a mountain. There he spoke to many people. He told them how to live as God's children. He said,
"Blessed are the peacemakers,
    for they will be called the children of God."
(Matthew 5:9)

Jesus wants us to work for peace. A person who works for peace is a **peacemaker**.

We are peacemakers when we say and do kind things for others. We work for peace when we try to get along with all people.

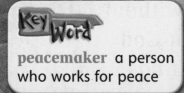

Key Word

peacemaker a person who works for peace

WE RESPOND

What will you do to be a peacemaker this week?

Act out one way you can share peace with one another.

We can make choices as children of God.

WE GATHER

✝ *Holy Spirit, help us as children of God.*

Think about some choices you made yesterday.
What games did you choose to play?
What did you choose for a snack?
What other choices did you make?

WE BELIEVE

God loves us very much. We are different from the rest of his creation. We are special. We can make choices.

We make choices everyday. Sometimes we make choices without even thinking about them. But God wants us to think about the things we say and do.

God asks us to choose to love him and others. He wants us to choose to do what Jesus taught us.

Here is a picture story. Circle the picture showing Tomás making a loving choice.

Tomás wants to use his sister's ⚽.

Tomás can choose to just take the ball. **OR**

Tomás can choose to ask his sister.

WE RESPOND

Do you think it is always easy to make choices that show love for God and others? Tell why or why not.

Pray together now.

Holy Spirit, help us to make loving choices.
Help us to do what Jesus taught us.
Help us to live as children of God.
Help us to walk always as children of
   the light.

**Circle the correct answer.
Circle ? if you do not know the answer.**

1. Jesus is the Light of the World.

Yes   No   ?

2. We show others the light of Christ when we tell lies.

Yes   No   ?

3. We are peacemakers when we fight.

Yes   No   ?

4. We can make choices to love God and others.

Yes   No   ?

 Talk about ways we can work for peace at home, in school, and in our neighborhoods.

 Make a booklet. On each page draw a picture of someone sharing the light of Christ with others. Write a sentence to tell what the person is doing.

We Respond in Faith

 ## Reflect & Pray

Trace over the letters. Now pray.

Jesus, I will share your light and peace with others.

Key Word

peacemaker (p. 213)

Remember

- Jesus is the Light of the World.
- We receive the light of Christ.
- Jesus asks us to share his peace.
- We can make choices as children of God.

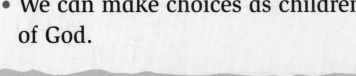 ## OUR CATHOLIC LIFE

Candlelight Prayer

In many places throughout the world, people gather to share Jesus' light by praying. They gather in churches, in halls, or even outside in neighborhood parks. People hold candles or other kinds of lights as they pray. We can join others in candlelight prayer. We come together to honor people who share in Jesus' light. We sing songs and pray together. We show that we are one family. We are all followers of Jesus.

SHARING FAITH
with My Family

Sharing What I Learned

Look at the pictures below. Use each picture to tell your family what you learned in this chapter.

Sharing Jesus' Gifts

Look at the candle. Color a section of the candle beside each thing your family can do to share Jesus' gifts of peace and light. Write your own ideas for other things you can do.

Pray together. Jesus, help us to share your light.

- Share what we have with others.
- Care about the way others feel.
- Say and do kind things.
- Try to get along with everyone.
- _____
- _____

Visit Sadlier's

www.WeBelieveweb.com

Connect to the Catechism
For adult background and reflection, see paragraphs 748, 1216, 2304, and 1730.

We Celebrate God's Forgiveness

19

✝ We Gather in Prayer

Leader: Holy Spirit, be with us now. Help us to think about ways we have or have not followed Jesus this week.

All: Holy Spirit, help us.

Leader: As I read these questions, pray to God quietly.

- Do I take time to pray?
- Am I kind to others?
- Do I listen to those who take care of me?
- Do I help people who need help?
- Do I tell the truth?

All: God, we are sorry for the times we have not loved you or others. Thank you for always loving us. We want to keep growing in your love.

Jesus told us about God's forgiveness.

WE GATHER

✝ *Jesus, thank you for teaching us about God's love.*

What is your favorite story?
Who is in the story?
What is the story about?
What happens at the end of the story?

WE BELIEVE

Jesus told stories to teach us about God's love and forgiveness. Here is one story he told.

📖 Luke 15:11–23

Read Along

A loving father had two sons. One day, the younger son asked his father for money. The son took the money and left home. He spent the money having fun.

Soon all the money was gone. The young man had nowhere to live and nothing to eat. He knew that what he had done had hurt his father. He wanted to go home and tell his father how sorry he was.

When the young man was near his home, his father ran out to meet him. He gave him a big hug. He was so glad to see his son again. The son told his father he was sorry. The father said, "Let us celebrate with a feast!" (Luke 15:23)

 Number these sentences 1, 2, 3 to retell the story.

_____ When the son was near home, his father came to meet him. He hugged him. They celebrated with a feast.

_____ The son asked his father for money. The son left home. He spent all the money.

_____ The son knew that what he had done had hurt his father. He went home to tell his father he was sorry.

Jesus told this story to teach us that God always loves us. God is like the forgiving father in this story.

WE RESPOND

Why were love and forgiveness important in this story?

God is always ready to forgive us.

WE GATHER

✝ *God, you are our loving Father.*

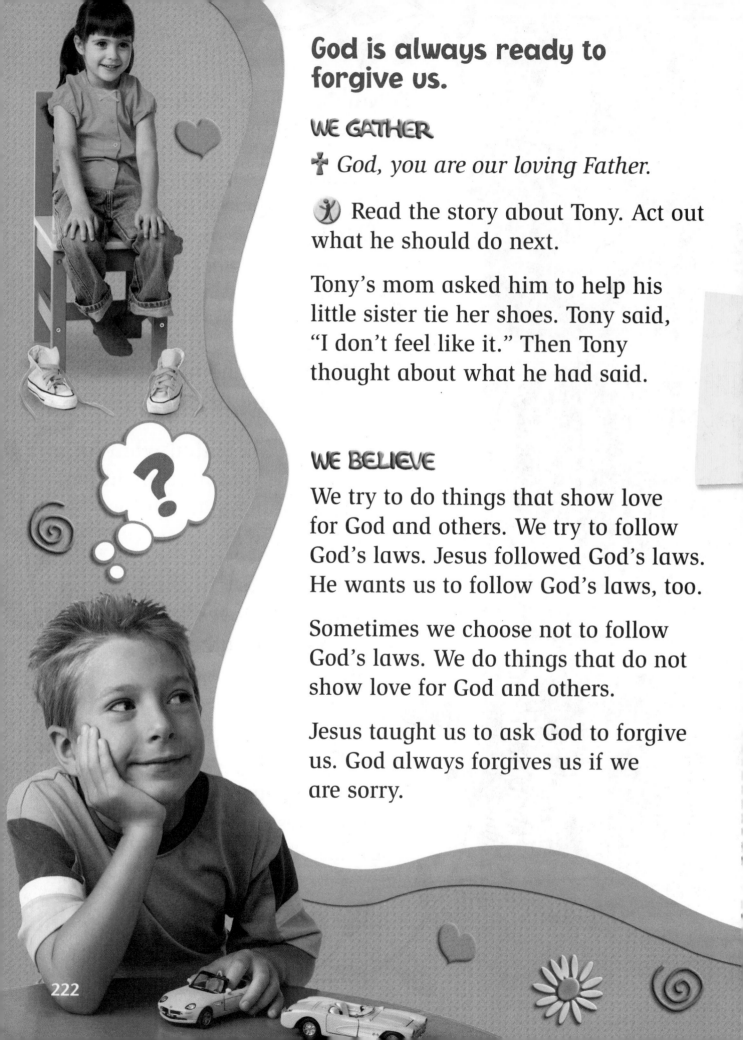 Read the story about Tony. Act out what he should do next.

Tony's mom asked him to help his little sister tie her shoes. Tony said, "I don't feel like it." Then Tony thought about what he had said.

WE BELIEVE

We try to do things that show love for God and others. We try to follow God's laws. Jesus followed God's laws. He wants us to follow God's laws, too.

Sometimes we choose not to follow God's laws. We do things that do not show love for God and others.

Jesus taught us to ask God to forgive us. God always forgives us if we are sorry.

WE RESPOND

God is always ready to forgive you.
How does that make you feel?

🎵 Children of God

Chorus

Children of God in one family,
loved by God in one family.
And no matter what we do
God loves me and God loves you.

Jesus teaches us to love.
Sometimes we get it wrong.
But God forgives us ev'ry time
for we belong to the (Chorus).

Jesus wants us to
  be sorry.
Sometimes we get
  it wrong.
But God forgives us
  ev'ry time
  for we belong to the
(Chorus).

223

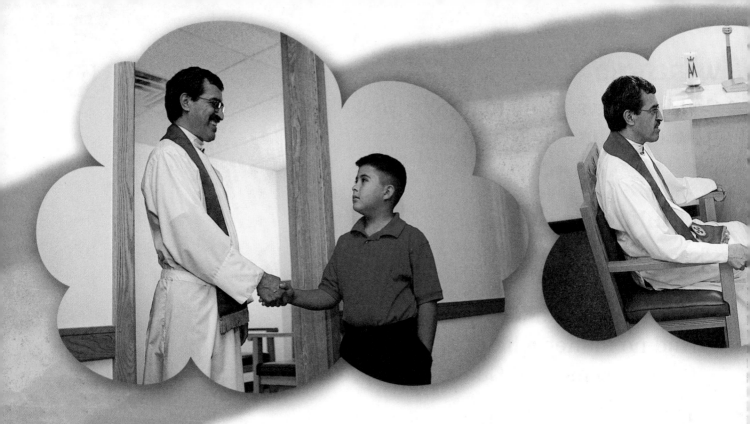

We celebrate God's forgiveness.

WE GATHER

✝ *God, thank you for your forgiveness.*

What are some ways to show others that you are sorry?

WE BELIEVE

When we make up with someone, we come back together again. This is called reconciliation.

We can always come back to God and ask for forgiveness. Jesus gave us a way to do this. It is the sacrament of **Reconciliation**. In this sacrament we receive and celebrate God's forgiveness.

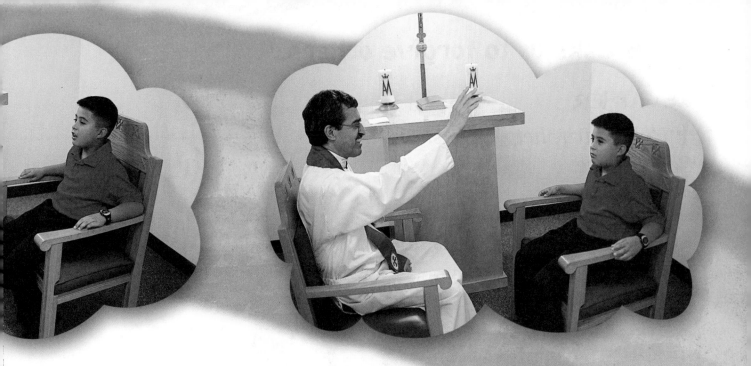

When we celebrate the sacrament of Reconciliation, we do these things.

- We think about what we have said and done. We are sorry for the times we have not loved God and others.

- We meet with the priest.

- We listen to a story from the Bible about God's forgiveness.

- We talk to the priest about what we have done. We tell God we are sorry.

- The priest shares God's forgiveness with us.

WE RESPOND

How can we tell God we are sorry? Talk to your family about God's love and forgiveness.

Reconciliation the sacrament in which we receive and celebrate God's forgiveness

As Catholics...

We usually celebrate the sacrament of Reconciliation in our parish church. There is a special place in church where we meet with the priest. Here we can talk with the priest face-to-face, or we can talk from behind a screen.

Where is the sacrament of Reconciliation celebrated in your parish church?

Jesus asks us to forgive others.

WE GATHER

✝ *Holy Spirit, help us to share God's peace.*

🏃 Look at the pictures.
Act out what you think is happening.

WE BELIEVE

When we celebrate the sacrament of Reconciliation, we receive God's forgiveness. We receive God's peace.

Jesus told his followers that it is important to forgive others. Jesus asks all of us to be forgiving. He wants us to share God's peace.

WE RESPOND

Ask the Holy Spirit to help you to be loving and forgiving.

Read the story.

Fran's little brother left her favorite book outside. It started raining. All the pages got wet.

Then Fran's brother said, "I am sorry, Fran. Please forgive me."

What would Fran say to be forgiving? Circle the words.

- "I am going to break one of your toys."

- "I loved that book, but I forgive you."

- "Go away. I do not want to talk to you."

Circle the correct answer.

1. Jesus told stories about God's love and _____.

forgetting　　　　　forgiveness

2. God is _____ ready to forgive us.

always　　　　　sometimes

3. In the sacrament of Reconciliation, we _____ and celebrate God's forgiveness.

receive　　　　　return

4. It is _____ to forgive others.

not important　　　　　important

 What are some things we do when we celebrate the sacrament of Reconciliation?

 Find a picture to show how people share God's forgiveness. Tell what you think is happening in the picture.

We Respond in Faith

Reflect & Pray

Show how you can thank God for his forgiveness and love.

Key Word

Reconciliation (p. 225)

Remember

- Jesus told us about God's forgiveness.
- God is always ready to forgive us.
- We celebrate God's forgiveness.
- Jesus asks us to forgive others.

OUR CATHOLIC LIFE

Sharing Stories

Some stories can be found in books and in movies. Many stories teach us the same lessons that Jesus taught.

Rainbow Fish is one of these stories. The writer, Marcus Pfister, tells a story about a selfish fish who does not have any friends. In the story, Rainbow Fish learns to share with others.

Talk with your friends about a story that you know that teaches an important lesson.

SHARING FAITH
with My Family

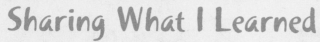

Sharing What I Learned

Look at the pictures below. Use each picture to tell your family what you learned in this chapter.

A Peace Plan

Talk about why it is important to make up with others when we have hurt them. How can each of these actions help?

- Say we are sorry.
- Talk over what we have done.
- Ask for forgiveness.
- Forgive others.

A Prayer for Forgiveness

God, we know that you always forgive us when we are sorry. Thank you for your love and forgiveness.

- For the times we did not listen to each other,
  please forgive us.

- For the times we have said things that hurt others,
  please forgive us.

- For the times we were not kind or caring,
  please forgive us.

Visit Sadlier's

www.WeBelieveweb.com

Connect to the Catechism
For adult background and reflection, see paragraphs 1421, 1431, 1440, and 2840.

A good samaritan

"Try to learn what is pleasing to the Lord."
Ephesians 5:10

The Church gets ready to celebrate Jesus' death and Resurrection.

WE GATHER

When do you remember what your family has done for you? When do you remember what God has done for you?

WE BELIEVE

Lent is a special time in the Church. We remember all that Jesus has done for us. We get ready for the Church's great celebration of Jesus' death and Resurrection.

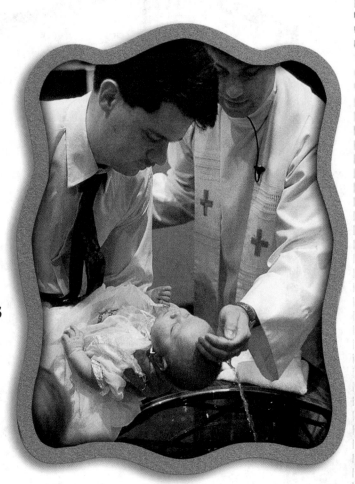

Lent is a time to remember our Baptism. In Baptism we first received grace, the gift of God's life. During Lent we praise Jesus for sharing his life with us.

We were baptized in the name of the Father, and of the Son, and of the Holy Spirit. Praying the Sign of the Cross reminds us of our Baptism.

Talk about the special things that happened at your Baptism.

Close your eyes. Thank Jesus for sharing his life with you. Now pray together the Sign of the Cross.

During Lent we try to grow closer to Jesus. We pray and follow his example. We thank God for his great love. We celebrate God's forgiveness. We help people who are sick, hungry, and lonely.

Followers of Jesus Christ should always do these things. However, they have special meaning when we do them during Lent.

Look at the pictures on this page. Act out what the people in the pictures are doing and saying.

WE RESPOND

Each time you do something to grow closer to Jesus during Lent, color one of the spaces in this cross.

✝ We Respond in Prayer

Leader: The Lord calls us to days of quiet time, prayer, and kind acts. Blessed be the name of the Lord.

All: Now and for ever.

Leader: During this time of Lent we trust in God's love and forgiveness.

All: Happy are those who trust in the Lord.

Leader: Together we pray as Jesus taught us.

All: Our Father, who art in heaven, hallowed be thy name;
thy kingdom come;
thy will be done on earth as it is in heaven.
Give us this day our daily bread;
and forgive us our trespasses
as we forgive those who trespass against us;
and lead us not into temptation,
but deliver us from evil.
Amen.

Sharing What I Learned

Look at the pictures below. Use each picture to tell your family what you learned in this chapter.

Growing Closer to Jesus

Lent is a time to grow closer to Jesus. Talk with your family about ways you can do this. Write one way on each leaf of this vine. Put your vine in a place where your family will see it often. Try to do some of these things during Lent.

Visit Sadlier's

www.WeBelieveweb.com

Connect to the Catechism
For adult background and reflection, see paragraph 540.

The Three Days

Lord, through your cross
you brought joy to the world.

The Church celebrates that Jesus died and rose to new life.

WE GATHER

Think about the crosses that you see. How are they different?

WE BELIEVE

Lent is a time that gets us ready for the Church's greatest celebration. Lent gets us ready for the great Three Days. These Three Days celebrate Jesus' dying and rising to new life.

During the Three Days, we gather with our parish. We celebrate at night and during the day.

We do the things Jesus asked us to do. We remember that Jesus gave himself to us at the Last Supper. We remember the ways Jesus loved and served others.

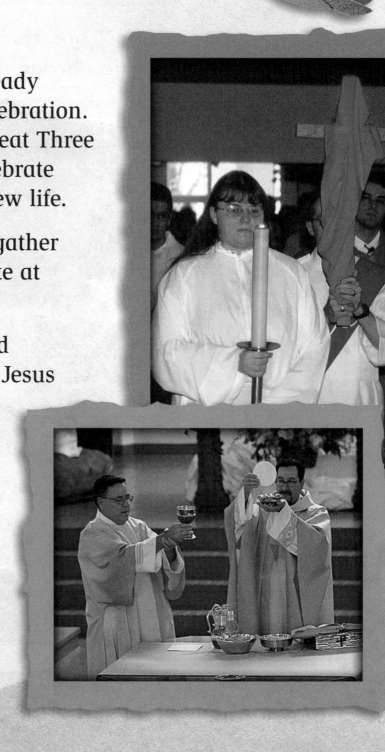

We listen to readings from the Bible. We pray before the cross. The cross reminds us of Jesus' dying and rising to new life.

👤 Draw a picture here to show one way you will celebrate the Three Days with your parish.

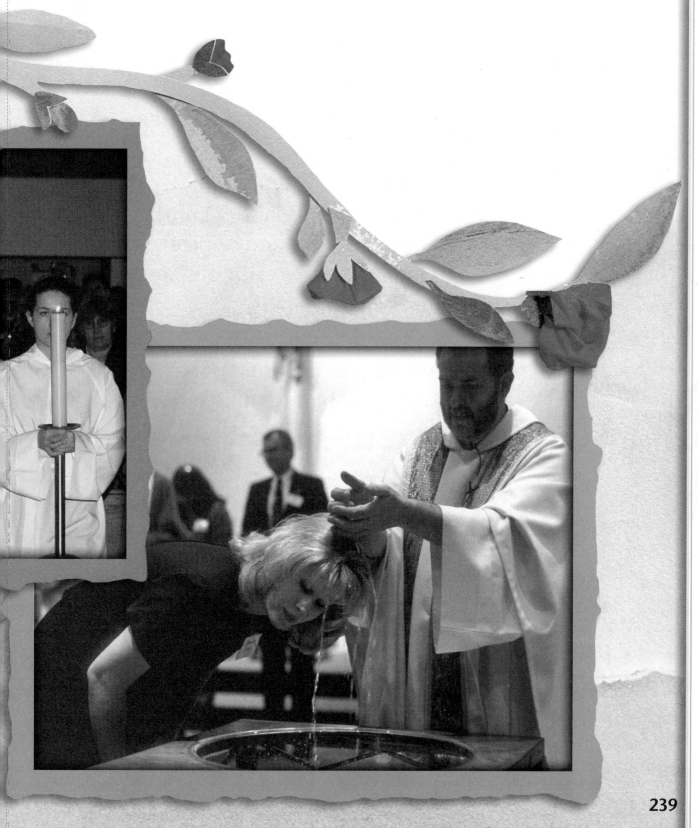

We sing with joy to celebrate that Jesus rose from the dead. We remember our Baptism in a special way. We welcome new members into the Church. We celebrate with songs of joy and praise.

WE RESPOND

♪ Awake! Arise, and Rejoice

Chorus
> Awake! Arise, and rejoice!
> This is the day of the Lord!
> Awake! Arise, and rejoice!
> Open the gates with our song!

> We sing now with Jesus,
> of love without end;
> we sing of the cross
> and of rising again. (Chorus)

HOLY! HOLY! HOLY!

✝ We Respond in Prayer

Leader: Lord, through your cross
you brought joy to the world.

All: Lord, through your cross
you brought joy to the world.

Leader: Holy is God!

All: Holy is God!

Leader: Holy and strong!

All: Holy and strong!

🎵 **Shout from the Mountains**

And we sing:
Holy, holy,
holy is God!
Holy, holy,
holy and strong!

HOLY!

SHARING FAITH
with My Family

Sharing What I Learned

Look at the pictures below. Use each picture to tell your family what you learned in this chapter.

The Three Days

The Church's celebration of the great Three Days begins on Holy Thursday evening and ends on Easter Sunday evening. Mark these days on your family calendar. Talk together about ways your parish celebrates on these days.

Visit Sadlier's

www.WeBelieveweb.com

Connect to the Catechism
For adult background and reflection, see paragraph 617.

Draw a line to match the sentence parts.
One is done for you.

1. Jesus is ● ● we use special words and actions.

2. Every week our parish gathers ● ● are called sacraments.

3. When we worship ● ● we receive the light of Christ.

4. The seven special signs Jesus gave us ● ● to worship God.

5. When we are baptized ● ● the Light of the World.

 Tell how a parish family worships together.
Tell how people in a parish work together.

Read the sentences below.

Use a ◖▬◗ **to circle the ones about Baptism.**

Use a ◖▬◗ **to circle the ones about Reconciliation.**

We are welcomed to the Church.

We tell God we are sorry.

We are invited to walk in the light of Christ.

Water is a sign of the life God gives us.

The priest shares God's forgiveness with us.

We Celebrate and Live Our Faith

UNIT 4 SHARING FAITH as a Family

Helping Children Make Good Choices

"**A**lways let your conscience be your guide," Jiminy Crickett sings to Pinocchio in one famous Disney movie. The development of a well-formed conscience takes time and guidance as we grow. Giving children the freedom to make their own choices isn't easy. Reminding them to consider the course of their actions can help.

Guide your child to consider the consequences. Now no one wants a little child to know first-hand what will happen if she or he plays on a busy street; it's just too dangerous. Smaller consequences, however, teach important lessons. The child who chooses to delay cleaning his room, for example, may lose precious playtime later on. Parents who hold to family rules and the consequences of not following them help their children weigh the pros and cons of a decision.

Help your child to consider the effect on others. Being a family essentially means being connected. One person's behavior can have an effect, good or bad, on others. When a child chooses to help set the table, for example, it eases the workload for someone else and makes the meal more enjoyable.

Ask your child to consider how it feels. Gauging one's feelings is a good barometer for measuring a decision's worth. Do I feel happy or sad? Generous or stingy? Satisfied or discontent? When parents pose such questions, it encourages reflective decision-making.

All of us need a voice of conscience to help us choose wisely. For now, yours will be the most influential in your child's life.

From the Catechism

"Parents should initiate their children at an early age into the mysteries of the faith of which they are the 'first heralds' for their children."
(Catechism of the Catholic Church, 2225)

Bible Q & A

Q: I want to read a Last Supper account to my child. How can I best explain the story to a first-grader?
–Los Angeles, California

A: Read Matthew 26:17–30. Use the passage to talk about family meals and about saying "goodbye" to friends.

Did You Know?

Over 106 million Americans have gone online. Here are the most popular things they do.

- send e-mail (93%)
- use a search engine to answer a question (80%)
- look for info on a hobby (79%)
- research a product before buying (73%)
- surf the Web for fun (68%)

(Pew Internet and American Life Survey 2000, www.pewinternet.org)

What Your Child Will Learn in Unit 4

Unit 4, the last unit of the year, celebrates the ways we can live out our faith in Jesus Christ. The meaning and order of the Mass and the celebration of the Eucharist are explained in terms first graders can understand and accept. After this presentation, the children will grow in their commitment to live out the Mass at home with your family. One way to enrich our experience of faith is to honor Mary, the Mother of God, and all the saints. The children will pray the Hail Mary as well as becoming aware of the ways the Church honors the saints. The last chapter of Unit 4 calls on the children to become more aware of our role as caretakers of God's creation. As we care for all of God's people, the children feel the Church commitment to welcome everyone.

Plan & Preview

▶ Have available sheets of drawing paper, crayons and markers. *(Chapter 23 Family Page)*

Razzle Dazzle Glitter

Jesus Gives Us the Eucharist

22

✝ We Gather in Prayer

Leader: Let us join hands and form a circle of friends.

Reader 1: O God, we gather now to pray.

All: We praise you together.

Reader 2: We listen to your word.

All: We praise you together.

Reader 3: We lift up our hearts.

All: We praise you together.

Reader 4: We share your love with everyone.

All: We praise you together.

Jesus shared a special meal with his followers.

WE GATHER

✝ *God, let us share in your life.*

 Think about a holiday celebration. Here are some things you do to celebrate. Finish the sentences using these words.

friends meal God family

Gather your ___ ___ ___ ___ ___.

Invite ___ ___ ___ ___ ___ ___ ___.

Have a ___ ___ ___ ___ together.

Thank ___ ___ ___ for this special time.

WE BELIEVE

On the night before he died, Jesus was with his followers in Jerusalem. They had gathered for a Jewish holiday. They were celebrating with a special meal. Jesus told them that he loved them.

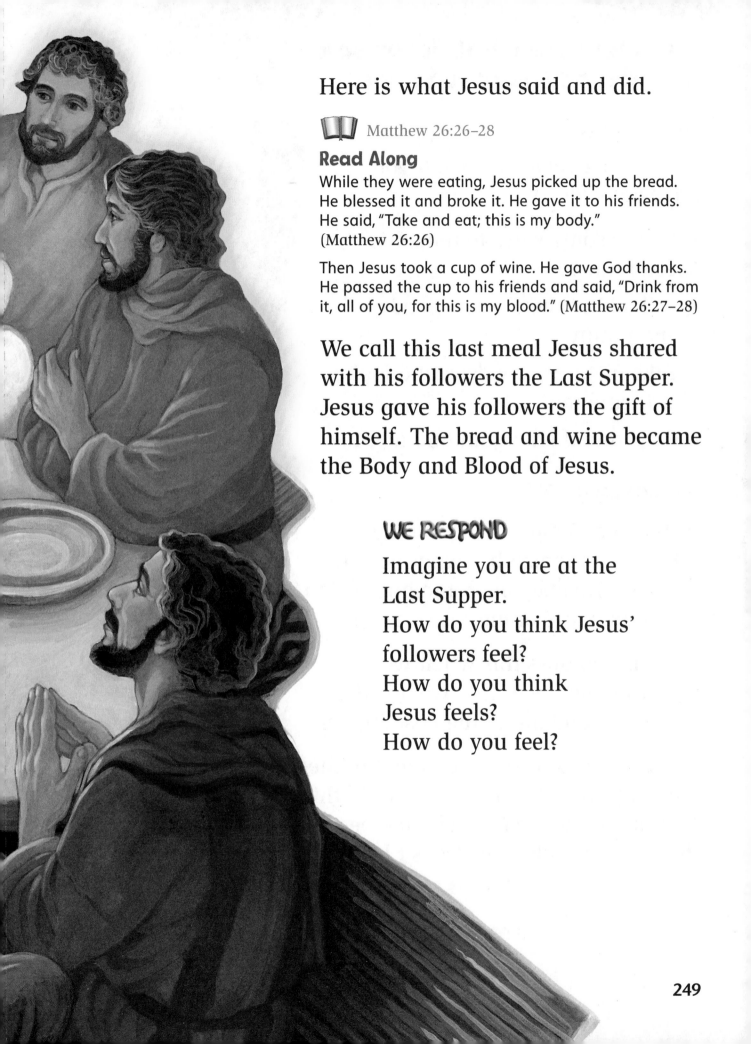

Here is what Jesus said and did.

📖 Matthew 26:26–28

Read Along

While they were eating, Jesus picked up the bread. He blessed it and broke it. He gave it to his friends. He said, "Take and eat; this is my body." (Matthew 26:26)

Then Jesus took a cup of wine. He gave God thanks. He passed the cup to his friends and said, "Drink from it, all of you, for this is my blood." (Matthew 26:27–28)

We call this last meal Jesus shared with his followers the Last Supper. Jesus gave his followers the gift of himself. The bread and wine became the Body and Blood of Jesus.

WE RESPOND

Imagine you are at the Last Supper.
How do you think Jesus' followers feel?
How do you think Jesus feels?
How do you feel?

We celebrate what Jesus said and did at the Last Supper.

WE GATHER

✞ *Jesus, we remember what you have done for us.*

Here are some ways to remember special times.

- Talk about them with friends and family.

- Take pictures or videos and look at them later.

- Celebrate them again and again.

WE BELIEVE

At the Last Supper Jesus told his followers to remember what he said and did. We obey his command to "do this in memory of me." (Luke 22:19)

The Church does this when we celebrate the Eucharist. We do what Jesus said and did at the Last Supper.

The **Eucharist** is the sacrament of the Body and Blood of Jesus Christ. In this sacrament, the bread and wine become the Body and Blood of Jesus Christ.

Key Word

Eucharist the sacrament of the Body and Blood of Jesus Christ

The word *eucharist* means "to give thanks." When we celebrate the Eucharist, we thank God for his many gifts. We thank Jesus for all he has done for us.

WE RESPOND

Pray quietly. Think of all the things Jesus has done for us.

 Finish this prayer.

Thank you, Jesus, for

_____

_____

_____

We celebrate the sacrament of the Eucharist.

WE GATHER

✝ *Jesus, thank you for the gift of yourself in the Eucharist.*

When do we worship God? What are some ways we praise and thank him?

WE BELIEVE

The **Mass** is another name for the celebration of the Eucharist. The Mass is the Church's greatest celebration.

At Mass we worship God together. We praise the Father for his love. We celebrate the life of his Son, Jesus. We ask the Holy Spirit to help us celebrate.

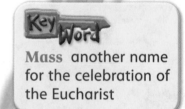

Key Word

Mass another name for the celebration of the Eucharist

Jesus is with us in a special way at Mass. He is with us when we gather together. He is with us when we listen to God's word.

Jesus is with us when we remember what he said and did at the Last Supper. He is with us when we share his Body and Blood.

WE RESPOND

Jesus is with us always. He is with us in a special way when we celebrate the Eucharist.

♫ We Come to Share God's Special Gift

We come to share God's
    special gift:
Jesus here in Eucharist
    for you, for me,
    for all God's family;
    for me, for you
God's love is always true!

We join with our parish for the celebration of Mass.

WE GATHER

✝ *Jesus, we celebrate your love for us.*

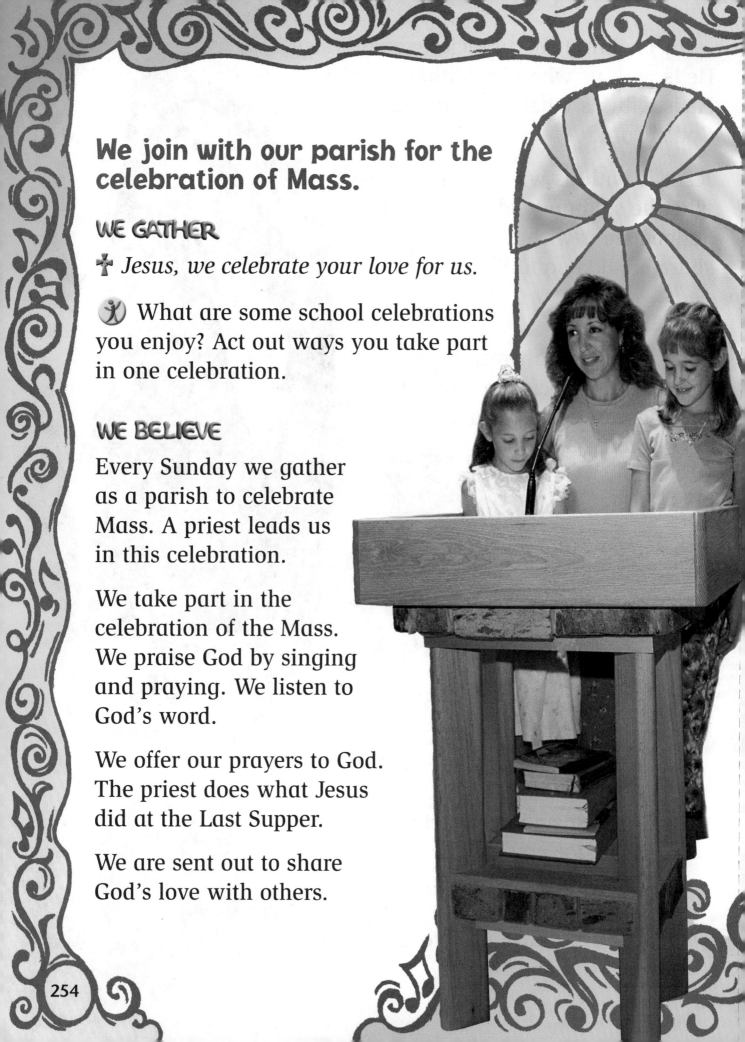 What are some school celebrations you enjoy? Act out ways you take part in one celebration.

WE BELIEVE

Every Sunday we gather as a parish to celebrate Mass. A priest leads us in this celebration.

We take part in the celebration of the Mass. We praise God by singing and praying. We listen to God's word.

We offer our prayers to God. The priest does what Jesus did at the Last Supper.

We are sent out to share God's love with others.

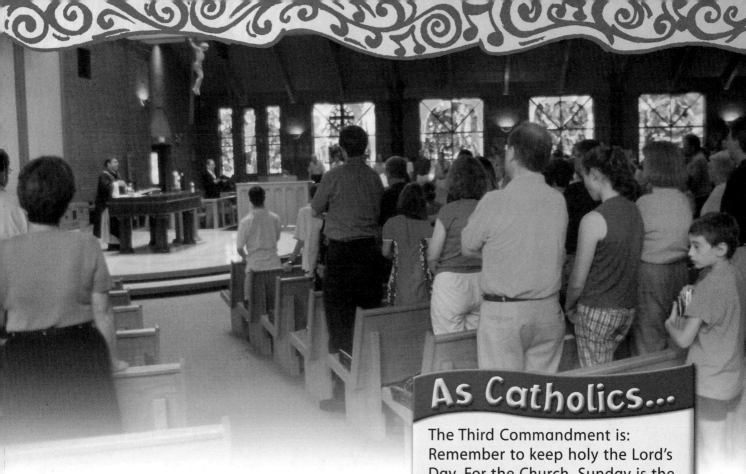

WE RESPOND

What can you do to take part in the celebration of Mass?

Three things you can do are hidden in the puzzle. Find and circle them.

```
P R A Y V W X Y
Z B X P S I N G
A L I S T E N J
```

At Mass this Sunday, do these things to praise God and remember his great love for us.

Use the words in the box to complete the sentences.

| Eucharist | Mass | meal | priest |

1. The Last Supper is the special

   _____ that Jesus
   shared before he died.

2. The _____
   is the sacrament of the Body and Blood
   of Jesus Christ.

3. The _____
   is another name for the celebration of
   the Eucharist.

4. A _____ leads
   us in the celebration of the Mass.

In what ways is Jesus with us
during the celebration of Mass?

Send a card to a friend. Use words
and pictures to tell about the ways we
remember what Jesus said and did
at the Last Supper.

We Respond in Faith

Reflect & Pray

Jesus, you are with us

Key Words

Eucharist (p. 250)

Mass (p. 252)

Remember

- Jesus shared a special meal with his followers.
- We celebrate what Jesus said and did at the Last Supper.
- We celebrate the sacrament of the Eucharist.
- We join with our parish for the celebration of Mass.

OUR CATHOLIC LIFE

Our Parish Celebration

The most important thing our parish does is to celebrate Mass together on Sunday. People of the parish give their time to help us celebrate.

Some people meet with the priest to plan the celebration. Other people greet us as we gather for Mass. During Mass, musicians, song leaders, altar servers, readers, and special ministers of the Eucharist help us to praise and thank God.

SHARING FAITH
with My Family

Sharing What I Learned

Look at the pictures below. Use each picture to tell your family what you learned in this chapter.

We Give Thanks

When we celebrate the Eucharist, we give thanks to God. We thank Jesus for all he has done for us.

Gather your family together. Use the letters in the word *eucharist*. Name gifts you would like to thank God for. You can add more, too!

Pray and thank God for his gifts together.

_____ E ACH OTHER

_____ U _____

_____ C _____

_____ H _____

_____ A _____

_____ G R ANDPARENTS

_____ I _____

_____ S _____

_____ T _____

Visit Sadlier's

www.WEBELIEVEweb.com

Connect to the Catechism
For adult background and reflection, see paragraphs 1339, 1341, 1346 and 2178.

We Celebrate the Mass

23

✝ We Gather in Prayer

Leader: Let us echo a
song of praise to God.

Glory to God in the highest, (Echo)
and peace to his people
on earth. (Echo)

We worship you, (Echo)
we give you thanks, (Echo)
we praise you for your glory. (Echo)

Glory
to
God

Glory
to
God

We gather to worship God.

WE GATHER

✝ *God, we worship you. We give you thanks.*

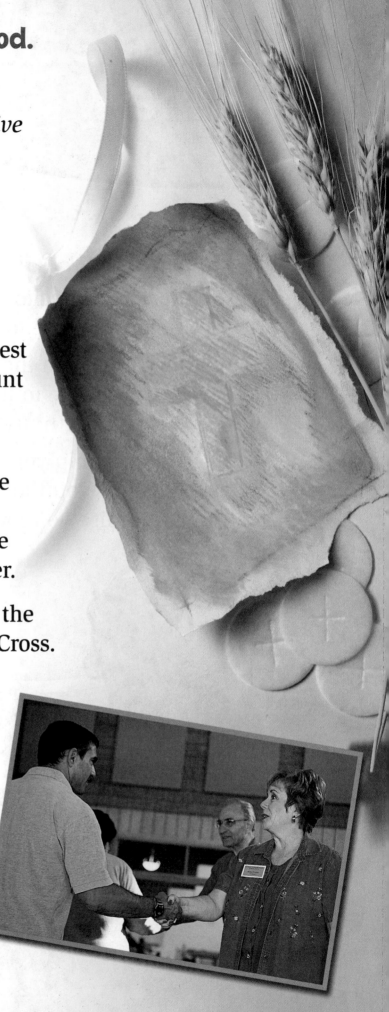

🧍 What are some ways we welcome people?
Act out some ways.

WE BELIEVE

The Mass is the Church's greatest celebration. The most important time that our parish comes together is for Sunday Mass.

As we gather, we welcome one another. We join together. We stand and sing. This shows we are happy to celebrate together.

The priest welcomes us. With the priest, we pray the Sign of the Cross. The priest says,
"The Lord be with you."

We answer together,
"And also with you."

These words remind us that Jesus is with us at Mass.

Then we ask God and one another for forgiveness.

We praise God by singing or praying aloud.
Our prayer begins:

"Glory to God

in the highest,
    and peace to his people on earth."

 Color the words that begin our
prayer of praise.

WE RESPOND

What are some ways the members of
your parish welcome one another as
the Mass begins?

Next Sunday, what
can you do to
take part in
the beginning
of Mass?

We listen to God's word.

WE GATHER

✝ *God, we praise you for your glory.*

🧍 When do you listen to stories from the Bible? Write who or what your favorite story is about.

_____

_____

_____

WE BELIEVE

The Bible is the book of God's word. At Sunday Mass we listen to three readings from the Bible. We listen carefully so that we may grow in God's love.

The first reading is about God's people who lived before Jesus Christ was born. The second reading is about the teachings of the apostles. It is also about the beginning of the Church.

After each of these readings, the reader says, "The word of the Lord."

We answer, "Thanks be to God."

Before the third reading, we stand and sing Alleluia or other words of praise. This shows we are ready to listen to the **gospel reading**. It is about Jesus Christ and his teachings.

The priest or deacon reads the gospel to us. Then he says, "The Gospel of the Lord."

We answer, "Praise to you, Lord Jesus Christ."

The priest or deacon talks to us about all the readings. We listen. We learn how we can grow as followers of Jesus. We learn how to be members of the Church.

gospel reading the reading at Mass about Jesus Christ and his teachings

After the priest's talk, we stand. We say aloud what we believe as Catholics.

Then we pray for the Church and all people. After each prayer, we say, "Lord, hear our prayer."

WE RESPOND

At Mass next Sunday listen carefully to the readings. How can you show others you have heard God's word?

As Catholics...

The word *gospel* means the "good news of Jesus Christ." The good news is that Jesus is the Son of God, who told us of God the Father's love.

Jesus taught us how to live. He died and rose to new life for us. This is the good news we celebrate.

What can you tell someone about the good news of Jesus Christ?

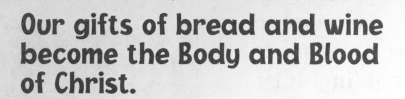

Our gifts of bread and wine become the Body and Blood of Christ.

WE GATHER

✝ *God, we offer ourselves to you.*

Think about the ways your family gets ready for special meals. How do you get the table ready?

WE BELIEVE

The **altar** is the table of the Lord. This is where we celebrate the Eucharist. With the priest, we prepare the altar. People bring gifts of bread and wine to the altar.

Everything we have is a gift from God. We offer these gifts back to God. We offer ourselves, too.

The priest prepares the gifts of bread and wine.
We pray,
"Blessed be God for ever."

Then we remember what Jesus said and did at the Last Supper. The priest takes the bread. He says,
"Take this, all of you, and eat it: this is my body which will be given up for you."

Then the priest takes the cup of wine. He says,
"Take this, all of you, and drink from it: this is the cup of my blood . . ."

The bread and wine become the Body and Blood of Christ. This is done by the power of the Holy Spirit and through the words and actions of the priest. Jesus Christ is really present in the Eucharist.

We sing or pray,
"Amen."
We are saying, "Yes, I believe."

WE RESPOND

Pray quietly. Thank Jesus for being with us in the Eucharist.
Then together sing or say "Amen."

Key Word

altar the table of the Lord where we celebrate the Eucharist

We grow closer to Jesus and one another.

WE GATHER

✝ *Jesus, we believe you are present in the Eucharist.*

What is the prayer that Jesus taught us? When do you pray this prayer?

WE BELIEVE

After the bread and wine have become the Body and Blood of Christ, we get ready to receive Jesus. Together we pray or sing the Our Father.

Then we turn to the people who are near us. We share a sign of peace. We say a prayer to ask Jesus for forgiveness and peace.

Then the priest invites us to share in the Eucharist. The people who have received first Holy Communion come forward to receive the Body and Blood of Christ. They answer, "Amen."

While this is happening, we sing a song of thanks. This shows that we are joined with Jesus and all the members of the Church. We grow closer to him and one another.

Then there is some quiet time. We thank Jesus for giving himself to us in the Eucharist. After this the priest blesses us.
The priest or deacon says,
"Go in peace to love and
    serve the Lord."
We say, "Thanks be to God."

We are sent to share with others the good news of Jesus. We go out to live as Jesus' followers.

WE RESPOND

What are some ways you can grow closer to Jesus?

🎵 We Come to Share God's Special Gift

We come to share God's
    special gift:
Jesus here in Eucharist
For you, for me, for all God's
    family;
For me, for you God's love is
    always true!

Circle the correct answer.

1. The altar is the _____ of the Lord.

table   home

2. The _____ is the reading at Mass about Jesus Christ and his teachings.

gospel reading   first reading

3. When we pray "Amen," we are saying, _____.

"Yes, I believe."   "Forgive me."

4. When people receive the Body and Blood of Christ, they say _____.

"Thank you."   "Amen."

 What are some things we do at the beginning of Mass?

 Tell what happens during Mass. Draw a picture or write sentences.

We Respond in Faith

Reflect & Pray

Jesus, at Mass I

Key Words

gospel reading (p. 263)

altar (p. 265)

Remember

- We gather to worship God.
- We listen to God's word.
- Our gifts of bread and wine become the Body and Blood of Christ.
- We grow closer to Jesus and one another.

OUR CATHOLIC LIFE

Praying and Serving Others

The parish always remembers those who are sick or unable to come to Mass. At every Mass we pray for the people who are not there. After Mass priests, deacons, or special ministers take the Eucharist to these people.

SHARING FAITH
with My Family

Sharing What I Learned

Look at the pictures below. Use each picture to tell your family what you learned in this chapter.

Celebration of Mass

Talk with your family about the special ways you each take part in the celebration of the Mass. Ask each family member to draw his or her picture taking part in Mass. Show your pictures to each other.

Pray or sing this song together as a family.

🎵 **We Come to Share God's Special Gift**

We come to share God's
    special gift:
Jesus here in Eucharist
For you, for me, for all God's
    family;
For me, for you God's love is
    always true.

Visit Sadlier's

www.WeBelieveweb.com

 Connect to the Catechism
For adult background and reflection,
see paragraphs 1348, 1349, 1353 and 1396.

We Share God's Love

24

✝ We Gather in Prayer

Leader: After Jesus rose to new life, he visited his followers. Let us listen to Jesus' words when he first visited them.

📖 John 20:19, 21

Reader: Jesus came and stood near them. He said, "Peace be with you."

(John 20:21)

All: Jesus, you gave us your gifts of peace and love.

Leader: Jesus told his followers that he wanted them to share God's love with everyone. We are followers of Jesus. He wants us to share God's love, too.

All: Jesus, help us to share your gifts of love and peace with everyone.

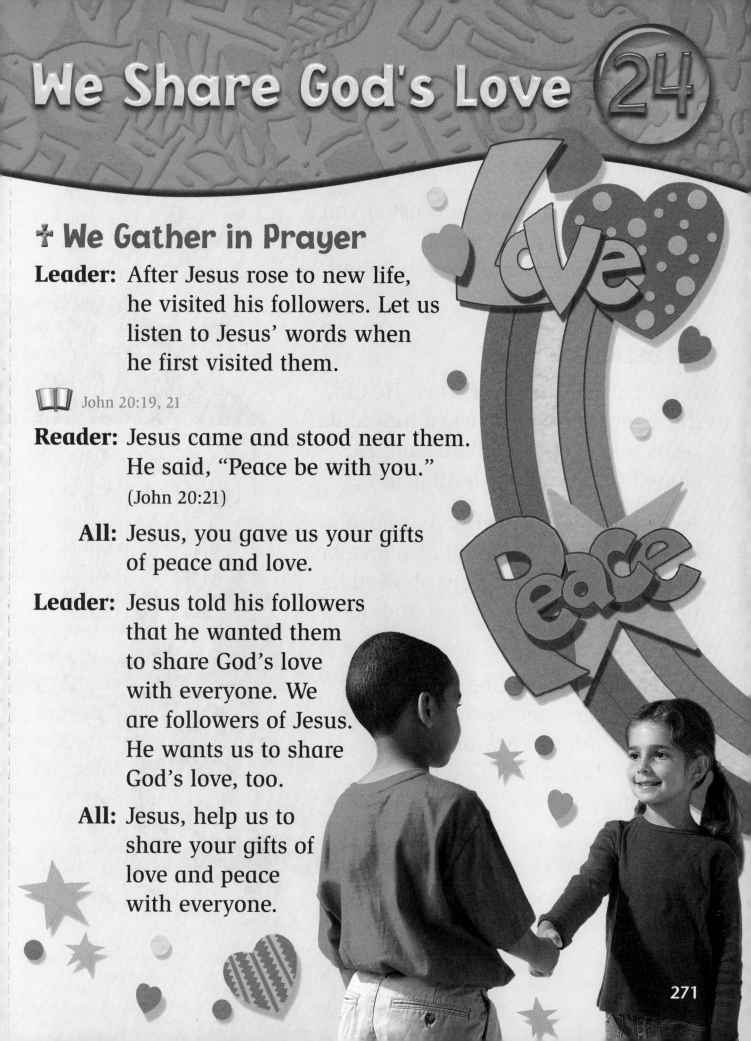

Jesus shows us how to love and serve.

WE GATHER

✝ *Jesus, help us to follow you each day.*

Think of a time someone trusted you to do something important.
How did you feel after you did what they asked?

WE BELIEVE

Jesus trusted God his Father. He did the things his Father asked him to do. Jesus told everyone about God. He shared God's love with all people.

Jesus told his followers, "As I have loved you, so you should also love one another." (John:13:34) Jesus showed us how to love and serve God and one another, too.

We love and serve God by learning the ways he wants us to live. We try to do the things he wants us to do. We tell others about God and share his great love.

Look at the picture. Tell how the people are loving and serving God.

WE RESPOND

What is one thing you will do to share God's love today?

273

When we pray, we show God that we love him.

WE GATHER

✝ *God, we want to be close to you.*

When do you talk to members of your family?
When do you talk to your friends?
What do you talk about?

WE BELIEVE

We spend a lot of time with the people we love. We talk and listen to them. We share what is important to us. We grow closer to each other.

We show God we love him when we pray. Prayer is listening to and talking to God. We grow closer to God when we pray.

Jesus taught us that God is his Father. He prayed to his Father often. He wants us to pray often, too. We pray to the Blessed Trinity: God the Father, God the Son, and God the Holy Spirit.

We can pray by ourselves. We can pray with our families, with our friends, and with our parish. We can use our own words to pray. We can pray the prayers of the Church.

As Catholics...

There are many ways to pray. We can praise God. We can tell God we are sorry for something we have done wrong. We can thank God for his loving care. We can ask God for what we need. We can pray for other people.

Try to pray in one or more of these ways today.

WE RESPOND

Write a prayer that you will pray this week.

____

____

____

____

We share God's love with our families.

WE GATHER

✝ *Thank you, God, for our families.*

What do members of your family share with one another?

WE BELIEVE

God wants us to love and serve him. We do this when we share God's love with our families.

We share God's love with our families in these ways.

- We are kind and helpful.
- We obey our parents and all those who care for us.
- We take care of the things that belong to our family.
- We show our love for all family members.
- We say we are sorry and forgive one another.

Look at the pictures. Act out what the family members are doing. Tell what they may be saying to each other. Talk about the ways each family is sharing God's love.

WE RESPOND

Think about the ways your family shares God's love.

How can you thank your family for sharing God's love?

We share God's love with others.

WE GATHER

✝ *Holy Spirit, help us to live as Jesus did.*

Have you helped someone this week? How did you help?

WE BELIEVE

God made each of us. He made us to share God's love with everyone. We can join with our own families to share God's love. We can join with members of our parish to do this, too.

Look at the pictures on these pages. Talk about what is happening in each picture. Tell how the people are loving and serving God.

WE RESPOND

Name one way you will help your family and parish serve others this week.

_____

_____

_____

🎵 **Walk in Love**

Walk in love as Jesus loved,
let us walk in Jesus,
light up the world,
light up the world
with God's own love.

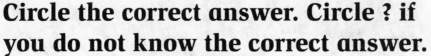

Circle the correct answer. Circle ? if you do not know the correct answer.

1. We serve God when we show others his love.

Yes   No   ?

2. We can pray only by ourselves.

Yes   No   ?

3. We share God's love when we forgive one another.

Yes   No   ?

4. We can serve God with other families and parishes.

Yes   No   ?

 **TALK ABOUT IT** How do we share God's love with our families?

 **ASSESSMENT** Make a poster titled "Loving and Serving God." Use pictures from newspapers or magazines or draw your own pictures.

We Respond in Faith

Reflect & Pray

God, I want to tell others about you. I

Remember

- Jesus shows us how to love and serve.
- When we pray, we show God that we love him.
- We share God's love with our families.
- We share God's love with others.

OUR CATHOLIC LIFE

Parish Priests

Parish priests serve God and others. They lead us in the celebration of the Eucharist and other sacraments. They talk with people who are sad or upset. They visit the people who are sick at home or in hospitals.

Some parish priests teach classes. They help people to learn more about the Bible and the Church. Priests also help people prepare to celebrate the sacraments.

SHARING FAITH
with My Family

Sharing What I Learned

Look at the pictures below. Use each picture to tell your family what you learned in this chapter.

Planning to Share God's Love

Get together with your family. Think of simple ways you can share God's love with the people on this list.

Keep the list in a place where everyone can see it. Then pray together. Ask the Holy Spirit to help you share God's love with all people.

Our Family

_____

People at Work or School

_____

People in Our Neighborhood

_____

People in Our Parish

_____

People of the World

_____

Visit Sadlier's

www.WeBelieveweb.com

 Connect to the Catechism
For adult background and reflection, see paragraphs 2196, 2558, 2217, and 1825.

✝ We Gather in Prayer

Leader: God chose Mary to be the mother of his own Son, Jesus.
Listen to God's word.

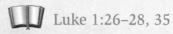 Luke 1:26–28, 35

Read Along

Before Jesus was born, God sent an angel to Mary. The angel said to Mary, "Hail, favored one! The Lord is with you." (Luke 1:28)
The angel told Mary that she was going to have a son. The angel told her, "The child to be born will be called holy, the Son of God." (Luke 1:35)

Leader: Joseph was Mary's husband. He loved and cared for Mary and Jesus.

♫ Joseph Was a Good Man

Joseph was a good man,
a good man, a good man,
Joseph was a good man,
chosen by the Lord.
And Joseph loved a lady,
Joseph loved a lady,
Joseph loved a lady,
chosen by the Lord.

Mary is the mother of Jesus.

WE GATHER

✟ *God, you give us people who care for us.*

 How do mothers care for and help their children? Act out some ways.

WE BELIEVE

God asked Mary to be the mother of his Son. Mary said "yes" to God. Mary gave birth to God's only Son, Jesus.

Mary loved Jesus. Mary cared for him. She helped him learn many things.

All through his life, Mary saw the wonderful things that Jesus did. Mary listened to Jesus teach. She watched him heal the sick. She celebrated special times with him.

Jesus always loved his mother. He wanted his followers to love and care for her, too. Mary shows us how to live as Jesus asks us to.

WE RESPOND

Jesus wants us to love his mother. How can we show our love for Mary?

The Church honors Mary.

WE GATHER

✝ *Holy Mary, pray for us.*

When we honor people, we show them how special they are to us.

Name someone you would like to honor. Tell why.

WE BELIEVE

The Church honors Mary. We honor her because she is the mother of Jesus. To show our love for Mary, we sometimes call her "Our Lady" and "The Blessed Mother."

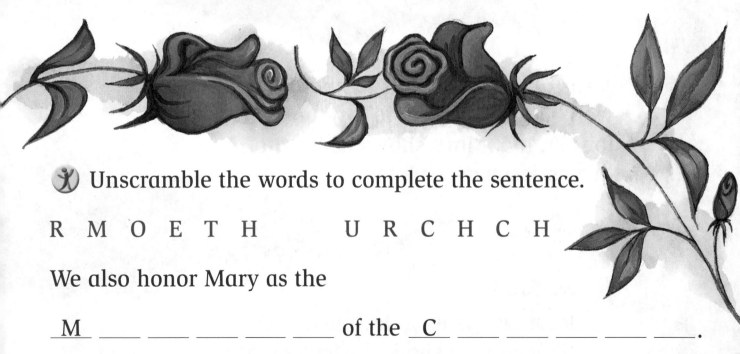

Unscramble the words to complete the sentence.

R M O E T H   U R C H C H

We also honor Mary as the

__M__ ___ ___ ___ ___ ___ of the __C__ ___ ___ ___ ___ ___ .

We honor Mary in different ways. One way is to celebrate her feast days. On these days, we remember special times in the lives of Mary and Jesus.

The Church also has prayers to honor Mary. We can say these prayers often. One special prayer that we say is the Hail Mary.

Hail Mary, full of grace,
the Lord is with you!
Blessed are you among women,
and blessed is the fruit of
    your womb, Jesus.
Holy Mary, Mother of God,
pray for us sinners,
now and at the hour of our death.
Amen.

WE RESPOND

Talk with a friend about ways you can honor Mary this week. Then choose one you will do.

Pray together the Hail Mary.

As Catholics...

We honor Mary in a special way on certain days of the year. On some of these days, parishes gather together for processions. On these special prayer walks, the people sing songs to Mary and pray special prayers. They put flowers in front of a statue of Mary. In this way they honor Mary.

Find out ways your parish honors Mary.

The saints are close to God.

✝ *God, keep us close to you.*

When you listen to stories about your family, how do you feel? What are some things you learn?

WE BELIEVE

The Church shares stories about many of Jesus' followers. Some of these stories are about the saints.

The **saints** are followers of Jesus who have died and now live forever with God.

The saints tried to live the way Jesus asked. They loved God very much. They tried to share God's love with others. They prayed to God often.

Saint Katharine Drexel began schools for Native American and African American children.

Saint Francis Xavier taught the people of India to know God.

Saint Andrew Kim Taegon was the first priest and pastor in Korea.

Look at the pictures on these pages.
They show some saints of the Church.
Read the sentence below each picture.

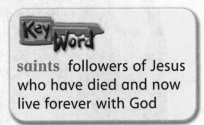 Use a yellow crayon.
Highlight each saint's name.

Talk about some people you know
who do the things these saints did.

WE RESPOND

Which of these saints can you be like?

Key Word

saints followers of Jesus who have died and now live forever with God

Saint Anne was the mother of Mary and the grandmother of Jesus.

Saint Teresa of Avila wrote books and letters to help people love Jesus.

Saint John Vianney was a parish priest who served his people.

289

We honor all the saints of the Church.

WE GATHER

✝ *Holy Spirit, help us to become saints.*

Look at the picture. The children are dressed as their favorite saints. Who is your favorite saint? Tell why.

WE BELIEVE

There are many, many saints.
We do not know all their names.

All the saints loved God very much.
They put God first in their lives.
They tried to be kind and fair.
They shared God's peace with others.

Saint John Bosco

Saint Mary Magdalen

Saint Peter

Saint Elizabeth Seton

The Church has a special day to honor all the saints. We call this day the feast of All Saints. This day is November 1.

On this day we gather with our parish family. We celebrate Mass. At Mass we thank God for all the saints.

All through the year, we can ask the saints to pray for us. We can ask them to help us grow close to God. We can honor them by trying to be more like them.

WE RESPOND

Tell some ways we can be like the saints. Ask the saints to pray for us.

♪ When the Saints Go Marching In

Oh, when the saints
    go marching in
Oh, when the saints
    go marching in
Oh, Lord I want to be in that number,
When the saints go marching in.

Circle the correct answer.

1. Mary is the _____ of Jesus.

mother   sister

2. A special prayer we honor Mary with is the _____.

Our Father   Hail Mary

3. _____ are followers of Jesus who have died and now live forever with God.

Saints   Sacraments

4. There are _____ saints.

many   one hundred

 **What are some of the things we do to honor Mary?**

 With a partner make up a prayer to honor Mary and the saints.

We Respond in Faith

Reflect & Pray

The saints lived as Jesus asked.
We can do this, too, by

Key Word

saints (p. 289)

Remember

- Mary is the mother of Jesus.
- The Church honors Mary.
- The saints are close to God.
- We honor all the saints of the Church.

OUR CATHOLIC LIFE

Saint Joseph

Saint Joseph was the husband of Mary and foster father of Jesus. He took care of Mary and Jesus. He was a carpenter in the town of Nazareth.

We ask Saint Joseph to help all the workers of the world, especially those who do work with their hands.

We celebrate the feast of Saint Joseph the Worker on May 1.

Sharing What I Learned

Look at the pictures below. Use each picture to tell your family what you learned in this chapter.

For All to See and Pray

Pray the Hail Mary often with your family.

Hail Mary, full of grace,
the Lord is with you!
Blessed are you among women,
and blessed is the fruit of
    your womb, Jesus.
Holy Mary, Mother of God,
pray for us sinners,
now and at the hour
    of our death.
Amen.

Visit Sadlier's

www.WeBelieveweb.com

Connect to the Catechism
For adult background and reflection,
see paragraphs 964, 963, 954, and 956.

We Care for the Gifts of God's Creation

26

✝ We Gather in Prayer

Leader: Close your eyes and sit quietly. Think about all the gifts of God's creation. Now let us praise God for all these gifts.

🎵 Shout from the Mountains

Shout from the mountains,
Sing in the valleys,
Call from the waters,
Dance through the hills!
All of God's people,
All of God's creatures,
All of creation,
Join in the song!

And we sing:
Holy, holy, holy is God!
Holy, holy, holy and strong!

The world is God's gift to us.

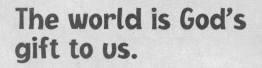

WE GATHER

✝ *Thank you, God, for all you have made.*

Close your eyes and picture yourself in your favorite outdoor place. Tell where you are. Tell what you see.

WE BELIEVE

God has given us all of creation to use and enjoy. The world is God's gift to us. It is full of beautiful places and wonderful plants and animals.

God asks us to take care of his creation. The gifts of creation are for all people. God wants people everywhere to be able to use these gifts. God wants us to share these gifts of creation.

Look at the pictures on these pages. Tell how the people are taking care of God's creation.

WE RESPOND

What are some ways you can share the gifts of God's creation?

 Draw a picture to finish this prayer.

God, we want to take care of the world. Help us to

Animals are part of God's creation.

WE GATHER

✝ *God, help us share the gifts of your creation.*

Look at the animals on this page. Where can you find these animals?

WE BELIEVE

God created the world and filled it with animals. Animals are wonderful gifts from God.

 Genesis 1:24–25

Read Along

"Then God said, 'Let the earth bring forth all kinds of living creatures: cattle, creeping things, and wild animals of all kinds.' And so it happened: God made all kinds of wild animals, all kinds of cattle, and all kinds of creeping things of the earth. God saw how good it was." (Genesis 1:24–25)

When God created people, he told them to watch over the animals.

We care for the animals when we make sure they have food to eat and water to drink. We also make sure they have a place to live. We try to learn more about them and what they need.

WE RESPOND

What animals can you take care of?

 Who are some people in your town who take care of animals? Write or draw about what these people do.

We are all important to God.

WE GATHER

✝ *We praise you, God.*

Find a partner. Tell some ways you two are alike. Name some ways you are different.

WE BELIEVE

God created each one of us. No two people in the world are exactly alike. We enjoy different things. We have different gifts and talents. We look different from one another.

God wants us to use our gifts and talents. We can use them to take care of creation and to care for one another.

WE RESPOND

What are your special gifts? How can you share them with others?

Let us thank God for making all people.

🎵 **Malo! Malo! Thanks Be to God**

(Sing each line two times)

Malo! Malo!
Thanks be to God!
O-bri-ga-do!
Alleluia!
Gra-ci-as!
Kam-sa-ham-ni-da!
Malo! Malo!
Thanks be to God!

As Catholics...

Each of us is special. God loves each and every one of us. He gave us the gift of life. We can show God our thanks for the gift of life. One way we can do this is by taking care of ourselves.

We can take care of ourselves by:

• eating the right foods

• getting enough sleep

• keeping ourselves clean

• obeying rules.

What other ways can we thank God for the gift of life?

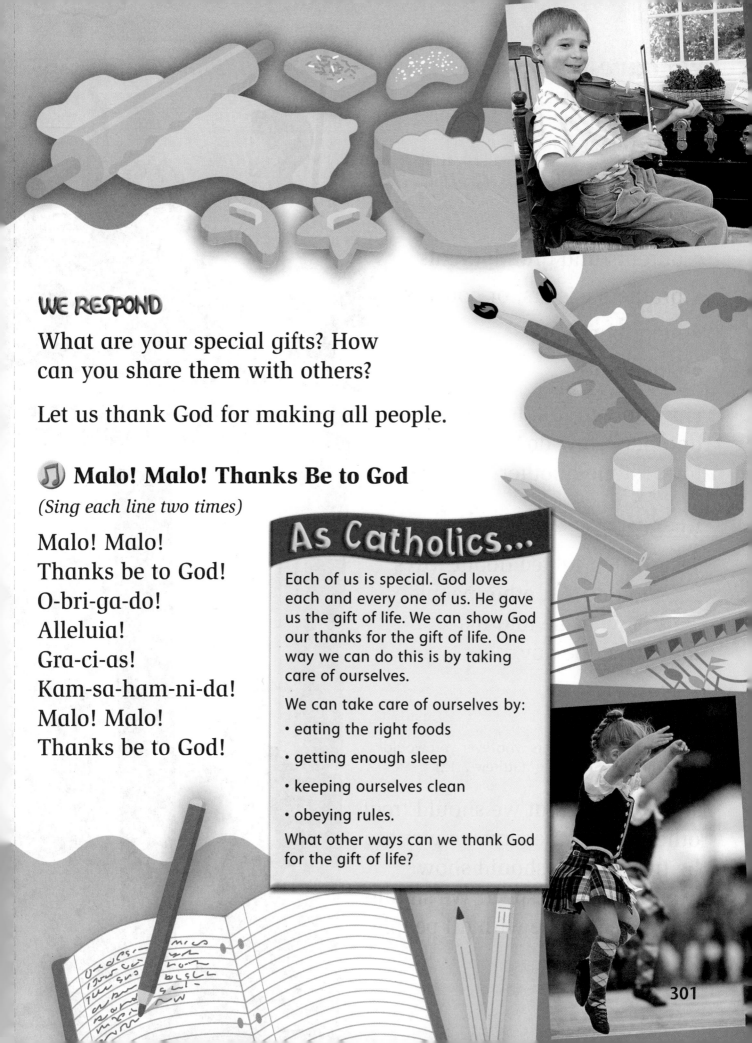

We care for and respect all people.

WE GATHER

✝ *Holy, holy, holy is God!*

Think about your:

- parents and grandparents
- brothers, sisters, or cousins
- neighbors
- classmates.

How do you talk to one another? How do you act toward one another?

WE BELIEVE

Jesus often talked about ways we should treat other people. This is what he told his followers one day.

 Matthew 7:12

Read Along

Jesus said, "Do to others whatever you would have them do to you." (Matthew 7:12)

Jesus meant that we should treat other people the way we want to be treated. We should show kindness and respect. We should share God's love with all people.

Here are some ways we can do this.

- Be polite. Say polite things like "Please" and "Thank you."

- Respect other people's belongings. Do not take anything without asking.

- Tell the truth. Do not tell lies.

- Ask for forgiveness if we have done something wrong. Say "I'm sorry."

- Forgive other people when they tell us they are sorry.

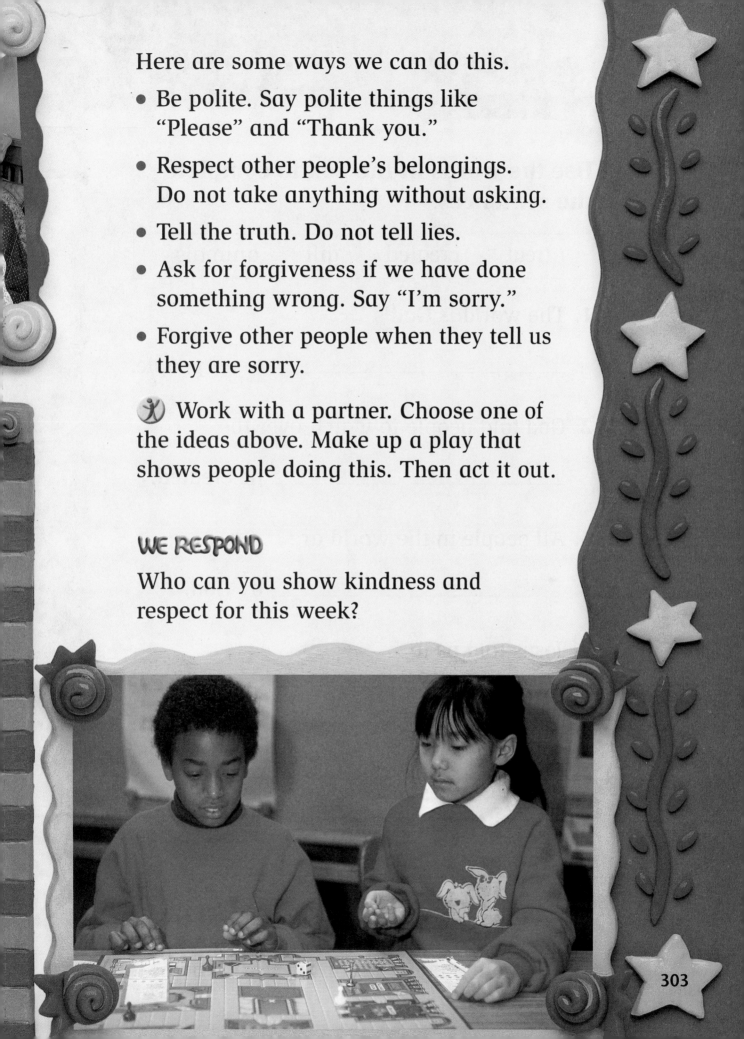 Work with a partner. Choose one of the ideas above. Make up a play that shows people doing this. Then act it out.

WE RESPOND

Who can you show kindness and respect for this week?

303

 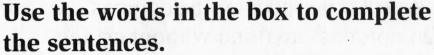

Use the words in the box to complete the sentences.

| treat | created | gift | animals |

1. The world is God's

_____ to all people.

2. God told people to watch over the

_____ he created.

3. All people in the world are

_____ by God.

4. Jesus told us to

_____ others the
way we want to be treated.

 How does Jesus want us to treat
other people?

 Make a poster to thank God for all
people and creation. Use pictures
from magazines or draw your own.

We Respond in Faith

Reflect & Pray

God, I will share the gifts of creation with

Remember

- The world is God's gift to us.
- Animals are part of God's creation.
- We are all important to God.
- We care for and respect all people.

OUR CATHOLIC LIFE

Tell your story here.

Place your photo here.

SHARING FAITH
with My Family

Sharing What I Learned

Look at the pictures below. Use each picture to tell your family what you learned in this chapter.

Gifts to Share

Gather your family together. Everyone has gifts and talents. Name some that God has given to each of you. Write them on the gift box.

Talk together about ways you can use your gifts and talents to help others. Then place the gift box on your prayer table.

Name	Gifts and Talents
_____	_____
_____	_____
_____	_____
_____	_____

Pray together:
Thank you, God, for all your gifts.
May we use them respectfully.
May we keep finding ways
to help your love grow.

Visit Sadlier's
www.WeBelieveweb.com

 Connect to the Catechism
For adult background and reflection,
see paragraphs 2415, 2416, 356, and 1825.

Easter 27

Advent | Christmas | Ordinary Time | Lent | Three Days | Easter | Ordinary Time

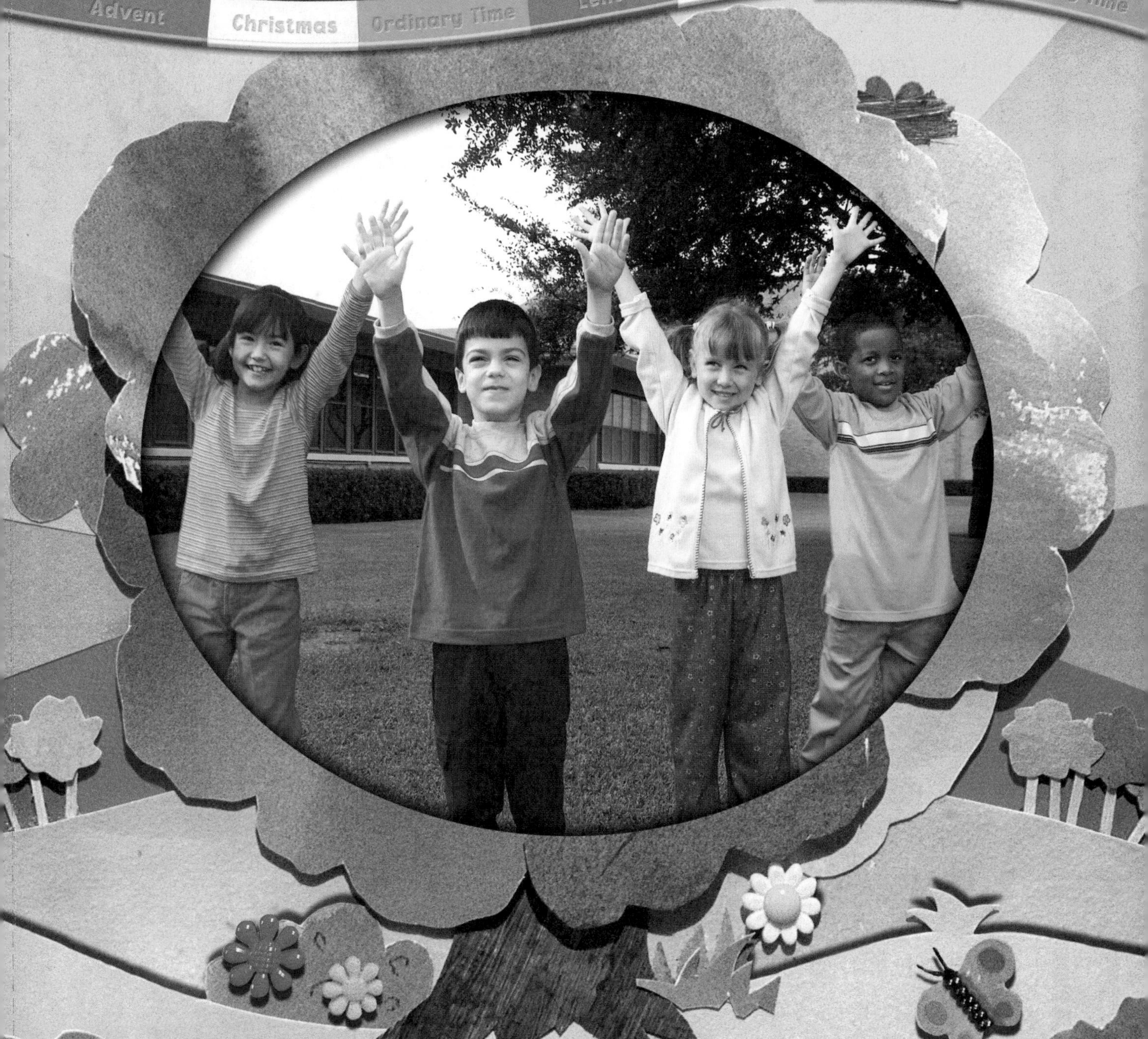

27

"This is the day the LORD has made;
let us rejoice in it and be glad."

Psalm 118:24

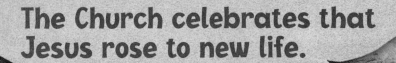

The Church celebrates that Jesus rose to new life.

WE GATHER

What are some signs of new life? Share your ideas with one another.

WE BELIEVE

Easter is a time of great joy. The Three Days lead us to Easter Sunday. It is time to rejoice!

During Mass on Easter Sunday, we listen to the story of Jesus' rising from the dead. Here is what Saint Matthew tells us.

 Matthew 28:1–10

Narrator: "After the sabbath, as the first day of the week was dawning, Mary Magdalene and the other Mary came to see the tomb. And behold, there was a great earthquake; for an angel of the Lord descended from heaven, approached, rolled back the stone, and sat upon it." (Matthew 28:1–2)

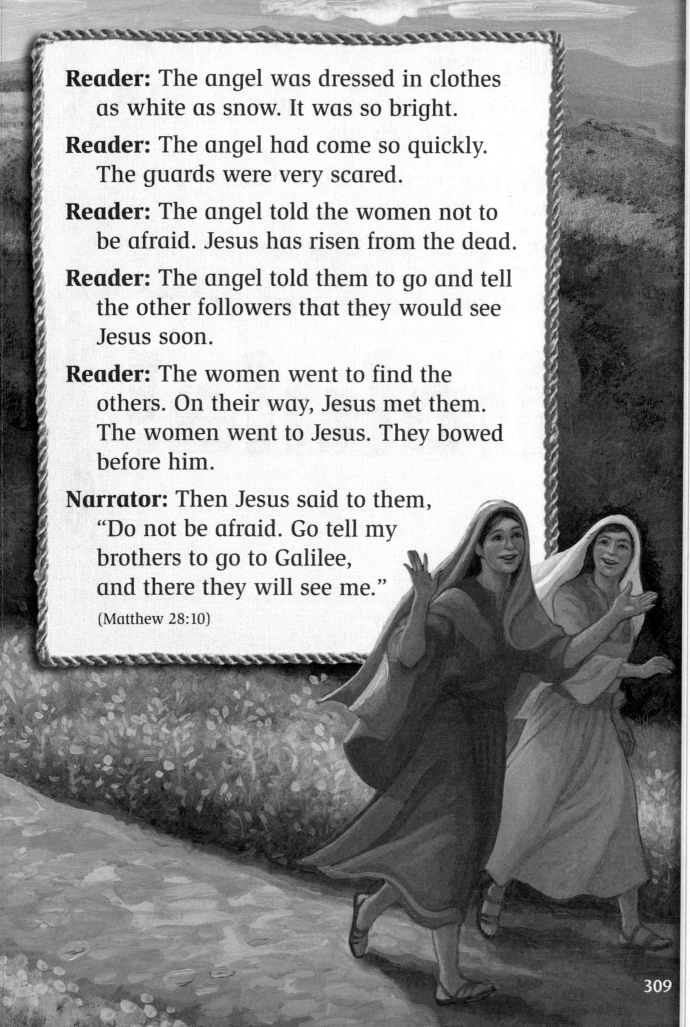

Reader: The angel was dressed in clothes as white as snow. It was so bright.

Reader: The angel had come so quickly. The guards were very scared.

Reader: The angel told the women not to be afraid. Jesus has risen from the dead.

Reader: The angel told them to go and tell the other followers that they would see Jesus soon.

Reader: The women went to find the others. On their way, Jesus met them. The women went to Jesus. They bowed before him.

Narrator: Then Jesus said to them, "Do not be afraid. Go tell my brothers to go to Galilee, and there they will see me."

(Matthew 28:10)

During Easter we celebrate that Jesus rose to new life.

🧍 Decorate the Alleluia banner with signs of new life.

Alleluia!

✝ We Respond in Prayer

Leader: Praised be the risen Jesus.

All: Let us rejoice and be glad, alleluia!

Reader: Christ has died,
Christ is risen,
Christ will come again.

All: Alleluia!

 **Alleluia No. 1**

Chorus
Alleluia, alleluia!
Give thanks to the risen Lord.
Alleluia, alleluia!
Give praise to his name.

Spread the good news o'er
all the earth:
Jesus has died and has risen. (Chorus)

SHARING FAITH
with My Family

Sharing What I Learned

Look at the pictures below. Use each picture to tell your family what you learned in this chapter.

Blessing of the Home During Easter Time

Leader: God fills our hearts and homes with peace. Blessed be the name of the Lord.

All: Now and for ever.

Leader: Christ risen from the dead is our hope, joy, and comfort. May all who enter this home find Christ's light and love.

All: Alleluia, Alleluia, Alleluia.

Visit Sadlier's

 www.WEBELIEVEweb.com

 Connect to the Catechism
For adult background and reflection, see paragraph 641.

SHARING FAITH
in Class and at Home

28

Read Along

Come and meet a family
    whose house is always neat.
They never spill a drop of milk
    or muddy up their feet.
They never get sad or mad or bored;
    they're cheerful without end.
It's a family you will never meet
    because they're just "pretend."

What makes the SuperStars
a "pretend" family?

Because *We Believe*

Jesus grew up in a real family.
He had to learn how to share
and get along with others.
Mary and Joseph helped
him learn.

We can be like Jesus when we
obey our parents. We can help
other people. We can forgive
each other.

We can be like the Holy Family.
We obey God's laws and show
our love for others.

How do we show we
believe this?

The SuperStar Family

"Whatever you do, in
word or in deed, do
everything in the name of
the Lord Jesus."

Colossians 3:17

Jesus did what Mary and Joseph asked him to do.

With Your Class

Talk about ways that Mary and Joseph helped Jesus learn. Draw one way here.

"The Christian family is . . . a community of faith, hope, and charity."

(Catechism of the Catholic Church, 2204)

With Your Family

Read page 313 together. Talk about the ways God wants families to love each other.

Tell a story about the ways your family shows love to one another.

Pray Together

O God,
Shower your blessings on this family gathered here in your name.
Amen.

(Catholic Household Blessings and Prayers [adapted])

NOW WHAT?
Bring this page back to School ☐   Keep this page at Home ☐

The Big Brother

Look at the picture. How can Brian help Sara as she grows up?

Because *We Believe*

When we are babies, like Sara, we need others to help us grow. We need help to learn how to be followers of Jesus, too.

Baptism makes us members of the Christian family. When we are baptized, we become children of God and members of the Church. Our families and other people in our parish teach us about God's love.

Baptized members of the Church help one another to follow Jesus.

How do we show we believe this?

Brian is going to help you learn a lot of things.

Sara, I'm your big brother, Brian.

"Live in love, as Christ loved us."

Ephesians 5:2

We can help others to follow Jesus.

With Your Class

On the computer screen, draw a picture that shows a way to follow Jesus.

Who helped you to learn this way?

With Your Family

Read page 315 together. Talk about the ways Baptism makes us members of the Christian family.

Name people who help children learn how to follow Jesus in these ways:

Thank God for his gifts.

_____

Share with others.

_____

Be kind and helpful.

_____

Who helped you to learn these things?

"Education in the faith . . . happens when family members help one another to grow in faith by the witness of a Christian life."

(Catechism of the Catholic Church, 2226)

Pray Together

Teach me, LORD, your way
that I may walk
in your truth.

Psalm 86:11

Making Choices to Share God's Love

Read these stories. Circle the one about a child who is choosing to share God's love.

- Michael gets a new video game for his birthday. He does not let his sister play it with him.

- Josie breaks a plate while she is fixing a snack. She tells her mother she is sorry.

Because *We Believe*

Jesus showed us how to love and serve God and others. He told us to love one another.

We can choose to act the way Jesus did. We can be kind and helpful. We can share. We can say we are sorry.

Jesus prayed to his Father. He wants us to pray too. We can ask Jesus to help us.

How do we show we believe this?

"Give thanks to the LORD, who is good."

Psalm 106:1

God wants us to love and serve him and others.

With Your Class

Talk about ways your class can love and serve one another. Write one way here:

_____

_____

"The Lord asks us to love as he does."

(Catechism of the Catholic Church, 1825)

With Your Family

Read page 317 together. Talk about the things we can do to share God's love.

Draw one way your family shares God's love.

Pray Together

Dear God,

We want to love and serve you.

Help us to

_____

Amen.

Circle the correct answer.
Circle ? if you do not know the correct answer.

1. The Eucharist is the sacrament of the Body and Blood of Jesus Christ.

Yes   No   ?

2. We call the celebration of the Eucharist the Mass.

Yes   No   ?

3. We should treat other people any way we want.

Yes   No   ?

4. The Church honors all the saints on the feast of All Saints.

Yes   No   ?

Write the correct word to finish each sentence.

world	Mary	saints	Lady

5. The Church honors _____

and the _____.

6. We call Mary "Our _____."

TALK ABOUT IT

Look at the pictures below.
Tell how the people are sharing God's love.
Act out what the people are saying and doing.

Draw one way you can share God's love.

My Mass Book

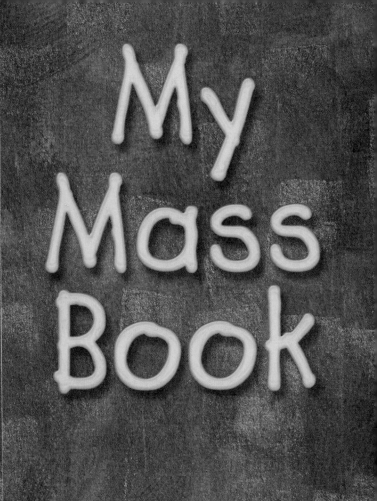

The priest blesses us. The priest or deacon says, "Go in peace to love and serve the Lord." We say,

"Thanks be to God."

We go out to live as Jesus' followers.

We welcome one another. We stand and sing. We pray the Sign of the Cross. The priest says, "The Lord be with you." We answer,

"And also with you."

We gather with our parish. We remember and celebrate what Jesus said and did at the Last Supper.

Fold on this line.

Cut on this line.

We ask God and one another for forgiveness. We praise God as we sing,

"Glory to God in the highest, and peace to his people on earth."

Then the priest invites us to share in the Eucharist. As people receive the Body and Blood of Christ, they answer,

"Amen."

While this is happening, we sing a song of thanks.

We get ready to receive Jesus. Together we pray or sing the Our Father. Then we share a sign of peace. We say,

"Peace be with you."

Fold on this line.

Cut on this line.

We listen to two readings from the Bible. After each one, the reader says, "The word of the Lord." We answer,

"Thanks be to God."

Then the priest takes the cup of wine. He says, "Take this, all of you, and drink from it: this is the cup of my blood. . . ."

We stand to say aloud what we believe as Catholics. Then we pray for the Church and all people. After each prayer we say,

"Lord, hear our prayer."

We stand and sing **Alleluia.**

The priest or deacon reads the gospel. Then he says, "The Gospel of the Lord." We answer,

"Praise to you, Lord Jesus Christ."

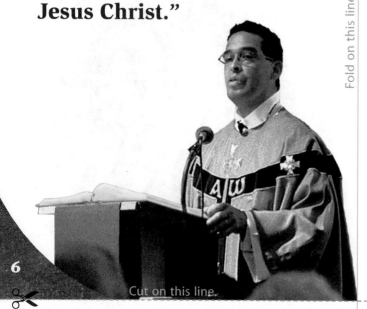

Cut on this line.

We sing or pray,

"Amen."

We believe Jesus Christ is really present in the Eucharist.

With the priest, we prepare the altar. People bring gifts of bread and wine to the altar. The priest prepares these gifts. We pray,

"Blessed be God for ever."

Then we remember what Jesus said and did at the Last Supper. The priest takes the bread. He says, "Take this, all of you, and eat it: this is my body which will be given up for you."

My Prayer Book

Fold on this line.

Cut on this line.

♫ Jesus Wants to Help Us

We believe Jesus wants to help us.

We believe Jesus wants to help us.

We believe that Jesus always wants to help us.

Glory to the Father

Glory to the Father,
and to the Son,
and to the Holy Spirit:
as it was in the beginning,
is now, and will be forever.

Amen.

Sign of the Cross

In the name of the Father,
and of the Son,
and of the Holy Spirit.

Amen.

Fold on this line.

When we pray, Jesus
wants to hear us.

When we pray, Jesus
wants to hear us.

We believe that Jesus
always wants to hear us.

Cut on this line.

Our Father

Our Father, who art
   in heaven,
hallowed be thy name;
thy kingdom come;
thy will be done on earth
   as it is in heaven.

He ascended into heaven,
   and is seated at the right hand
   of the Father.
He will come again to judge
   the living and the dead.

I believe in the Holy Spirit,
   the holy catholic Church,
   the communion of saints,
   the forgiveness of sins,
   the resurrection of the body,
   and the life everlasting.

Amen.

The Apostles' Creed

Read Along

I believe in God the
  Father almighty,
  creator of heaven and earth.

I believe in Jesus Christ,
  his only Son, our Lord.
  He was conceived by the power
  of the Holy Spirit
  and born of the Virgin Mary.
  He suffered under Pontius Pilate,
  was crucified, died and
  was buried.
  He descended to the dead.
  On the third day he rose again.

Give us this day our
  daily bread;
and forgive us our
  trespasses
as we forgive those who
  trespass against us;
and lead us not into
  temptation,
but deliver us from evil.

Amen.

Fold on this line.

Cut on this line.

Grace Before Meals

Bless us, O Lord, and these
  your gifts
which we are about
  to receive
from your goodness.
Through Christ our Lord.

Amen.

Holy Mary, mother of God,
pray for us sinners,
now and at the hour of
  our death.

Amen.

Hail Mary

Hail Mary, full of grace,
the Lord is with you!
Blessed are you among
    women,
and blessed is the fruit of
    your womb, Jesus.

Fold on this line.

Grace After Meals

We give you thanks
    almighty God
for these and all your gifts,
which we have received
    through
Christ our Lord.

Amen.

Cut on this line.

Morning Offering

My God, I offer you today
all that I think and do
    and say,
uniting it with what
    was done
on earth, by Jesus Christ,
your Son.

Evening Prayer

Dear God, before I sleep
I want to thank you for
    this day
so full of your kindness
and your joy.
I close my eyes to rest
safe in your loving care.

The Seven Sacraments

The Sacraments of Christian Initiation

Baptism

Confirmation

Eucharist

The Sacraments of Healing

Penance and Reconciliation

Anointing of the Sick

The Sacraments at the Service of Communion

Holy Orders

Matrimony

The Ten Commandments

1. I am the LORD your God: you shall not have strange gods before me.

2. You shall not take the name of the LORD your God in vain.

3. Remember to keep holy the LORD's Day.

4. Honor your father and your mother.

5. You shall not kill.

6. You shall not commit adultery.

7. You shall not steal.

8. You shall not bear false witness against your neighbor.

9. You shall not covet your neighbor's wife.

10. You shall not covet your neighbor's goods.

Glossary

altar (page 265)
the table of the Lord where we celebrate the Eucharist

apostles (page 97)
twelve men Jesus chose to lead his followers

Baptism (page 196)
the sacrament in which we become children of God and members of the Church

Bible (page 21)
the book of God's word

Blessed Trinity (page 36)
one God in the three Persons: God the Father, God the Son, and God the Holy Spirit

Christmas (page 47)
the time when we celebrate the birth of God's Son, Jesus

Church (page 133)
all the people who believe in Jesus and follow his teachings

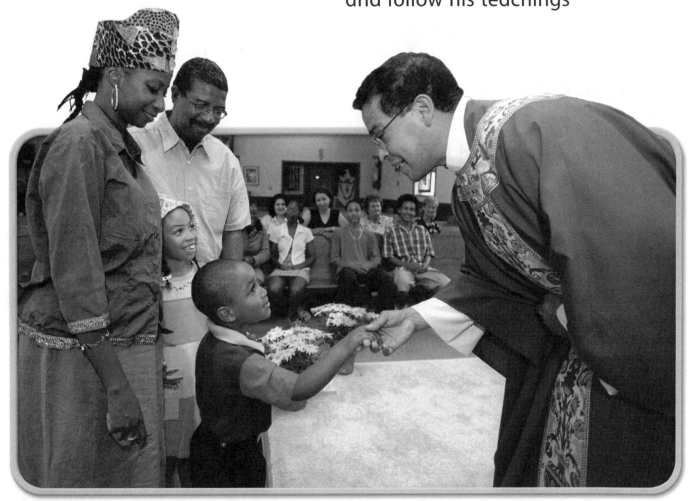

Lord's Prayer (page 101)
the prayer Jesus taught his followers

Mass (page 252)
another name for the celebration of the Eucharist

parish (page 173)
a group of Catholics who join together to share God's love

pastor (page 176)
the priest who is the leader of the parish

peacemaker (page 213)
a person who works for peace

Pentecost (page 125)
the day the Holy Spirit came to Jesus' followers

prayer (page 39)
listening and talking to God

Reconciliation (page 225)
the sacrament in which we receive and celebrate God's forgiveness

sacrament (page 189)
a special sign given to us by Jesus

saints (page 289)
followers of Jesus who have died and now live forever with God

Sign of the Cross (page 39)
a prayer to the Blessed Trinity

Temple (page 113)
the holy place in Jerusalem where the Jewish people prayed

trust (page 61)
to believe in someone's love for us

worship (page 175)
to give God thanks and praise

Index

The following is a list of topics that appear in the pupil's text.
Boldface indicates an entire chapter.

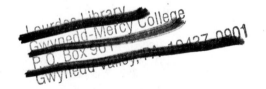